Living Faith

New Testament Theology

Edited by Thomas R. Schreiner and Brian S. Rosner

The Beginning of the Gospel: A Theology of Mark, Peter Orr

From the Manger to the Throne: A Theology of Luke, Benjamin L. Gladd

The Mission of the Triune God: A Theology of Acts, Patrick Schreiner

Strengthened by the Gospel: A Theology of Romans, Brian S. Rosner

Ministry in the New Realm: A Theology of 2 Corinthians, Dane C. Ortlund

Christ Crucified: A Theology of Galatians, Thomas R. Schreiner

United to Christ, Walking in the Spirit: A Theology of Ephesians, Benjamin L. Merkle

Sharing Christ in Joy and Sorrow: A Theology of Philippians, Chris Bruno

Hidden with Christ in God: A Theology of Colossians and Philemon, Kevin W. McFadden

To Walk and to Please God: A Theology of 1 and 2 Thessalonians, Andrew S. Malone

The Appearing of God Our Savior: A Theology of 1 and 2 Timothy and Titus, Claire S. Smith

Perfect Priest for Weary Pilgrims: A Theology of Hebrews, Dennis E. Johnson

Living Faith: A Theology of James, Robert L. Plummer

The God Who Judges and Saves: A Theology of 2 Peter and Jude, Matthew S. Harmon

The Joy of Hearing: A Theology of the Book of Revelation, Thomas R. Schreiner

"Some biblical books have literary forms that make them difficult to grasp in the verse-by-verse format of a commentary and, thus, need a thematic, theological exposition. That is what Robert Plummer has done for James, laying out its teaching logically and clearly in the best tradition of evangelical biblical studies. He avoids side issues that would distract from the main themes and makes those main themes clear for lay reader and scholar alike. For that I congratulate him."

Peter H. Davids, Chaplain, Our Lady of Guadalupe Priory, Houston, Texas

"Robert Plummer offers an accessible analysis of the epistle of James. He shows that it is not an epistle of straw but an epistle for those who need to do more in their faith to follow in the way of Jesus's teachings. He explains how James provides instruction on a living faith that seeks wisdom from above, endures trials, spurns the trappings of wealth, speaks without anger, perseveres in prayer, and keeps Jesus's command to love one another."

Michael F. Bird, Deputy Principal, Ridley College

"Robert Plummer's theology of the book of James is both scholarly and accessible, reminding the reader that genuine faith is a living faith. Themes such as faith and works, trials and temptations, and poverty and riches are explored not only in this letter but also within the broader narrative of Scripture. A great resource for those pursuing greater biblical and theological insights from this epistle."

Roger Severino, Leadership Development Minister, Brentwood Baptist Church, Brentwood, Tennessee

"An influential German commentator once declared that James has no theology. Robert Plummer has laid to rest any such idea. By expanding our definition of theology to include biblical teaching that is firmly grounded in an understanding of God and his saving purposes, Plummer has clearly demonstrated that James most certainly has a theology! James speaks of the Father and the Son and many of the traditional doctrines that embody the Christian faith."

William Varner, Professor of Biblical Studies, The Master's University; author, *James: An Exegetical Commentary* and *James: A Devotional Commentary*

"The title *Living Faith* says it all: The book of James captures both a faith that is alive and a faith that enables living rightly in our day. Robert Plummer unpacks the theology of James, depicting a faith that is vibrant, dynamic, and yet intensely practical. *Living Faith* explores the great themes of James—faith and works, trials and temptations, poverty and riches, speech and anger, and, most importantly, prayer—to issue a compelling call for a faith that reveals the reality of one's salvation through obedience to Jesus Christ and deeds motivated by his word and Spirit. As a former student in Plummer's class on the exegesis of James, I know that his engaging exposition of James rings true because Plummer's life, ministry, and teaching are a beacon to the trustworthiness of his Savior who inspires such faith in his followers."

Robert B. Crotty, Men's Equipping Director, Watermark Community Church, Dallas, Texas

"The outstanding feature of Robert Plummer's study *Living Faith* is its combination of scholarly depth and pastoral insight. He reveals the letter of James as 'a faithful recapitulation of Jesus's teachings,' emphasizing the necessity for true believers to demonstrate a living faith through observable acts of obedience and love. The first two chapters are true gems, particularly insightful, enriching readers' understanding and appreciation of the letter. Plummer's work is invaluable and most timely."

Patrick J. Hartin, Professor Emeritus of Religious Studies, Gonzaga University; author, *James and the "Q" Sayings of Jesus*; *Sacra Pagina: James*; and *A Spirituality of Perfection*

Living Faith

A Theology of James

Robert L. Plummer

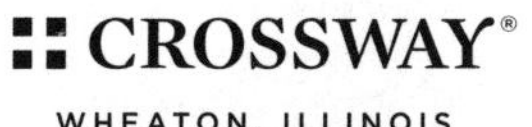

WHEATON, ILLINOIS

Living Faith: A Theology of James

Published by Crossway
1300 Crescent Street
Wheaton, Illinois 60187

Cover design: Kevin Lipp

First printing 2025

Printed in the United States of America

All emphases in Scripture quotations have been added by the author.

Trade paperback ISBN: 978-1-4335-7419-1
ePub ISBN: 978-1-4335-7422-1
PDF ISBN: 978-1-43351-7420-7

Library of Congress Cataloging-in-Publication Data

Names: Plummer, Robert L. (Robert Lewis), 1971- author.
Title: Living faith : a theology of James / Robert L. Plummer.
Description: Wheaton, Illinois : Crossway, 2025. | Series: New Testament theology | Includes bibliographical references and index.
Identifiers: LCCN 2024045086 (print) | LCCN 2024045087 (ebook) | ISBN 9781433574191 (trade paperback) | ISBN 9781433574207 (pdf) | ISBN 9781433574221 (epub)
Subjects: LCSH: Bible. James—Commentaries.
Classification: LCC BS2785.53 .P38 2025 (print) | LCC BS2785.53 (ebook) | DDC 227/.9107—dc23/eng/20250602
LC record available at https://lccn.loc.gov/2024045086
LC ebook record available at https://lccn.loc.gov/2024045087

Crossway is a publishing ministry of Good News Publishers.

VP 34 33 32 31 30 29 28 27 26 25
15 14 13 12 11 10 9 8 7 6 5 4 3 2 1

To my dear mother,
Sonja Plummer,
a woman who
has living faith

Faith is not the human notion and dream that some people call faith. When they see that no improvement of life and no good works follow—although they can hear and say much about faith—they fall into the error of saying, "Faith is not enough; one must do works in order to be righteous and be saved." This is due to the fact that when they hear the gospel, they get busy and by their own powers create an idea in their heart which says, "I believe"; they take this then to be a true faith. But, as it is a human figment and idea that never reaches the depths of the heart, nothing comes of it either, and no improvement follows.

Faith, however, is a divine work in us which changes us and makes us to be born anew of God, John 1[:12–13]. It kills the old Adam and makes us altogether different men, in heart and spirit and mind and powers; and it brings with it the Holy Spirit. O it is a living, busy, active mighty thing, this faith. It is impossible for it not to be doing good works incessantly. It does not ask whether good works are to be done, but before the question is asked, it has already done them, and is constantly doing them. Whoever does not do such works, however, is an unbeliever. He gropes and looks around for faith and good works, but knows neither what faith is nor what good works are. Yet he talks and talks, with many words, about faith and good works.

MARTIN LUTHER, "PREFACE TO THE EPISTLE OF ST. PAUL TO THE ROMANS"

Contents

Series Preface

THERE ARE REMARKABLY few treatments of the big ideas of single books of the New Testament. Readers can find brief coverage in Bible dictionaries, in some commentaries, and in New Testament theologies, but such books are filled with other information and are not devoted to unpacking the theology of each New Testament book in its own right. Technical works concentrating on various themes of New Testament theology often have a narrow focus, treating some aspect of the teaching of, say, Matthew or Hebrews in isolation from the rest of the book's theology.

The New Testament Theology series seeks to fill this gap by providing students of Scripture with readable book-length treatments of the distinctive teaching of each New Testament book or collection of books. The volumes approach the text from the perspective of biblical theology. They pay due attention to the historical and literary dimensions of the text, but their main focus is on presenting the teaching of particular New Testament books about God and his relations to the world on their own terms, maintaining sight of the Bible's overarching narrative and Christocentric focus. Such biblical theology is of fundamental importance to biblical and expository preaching and informs exegesis, systematic theology, and Christian ethics.

The twenty volumes in the series supply comprehensive, scholarly, and accessible treatments of theological themes from an evangelical perspective. We envision them being of value to students, preachers, and interested laypeople. When preparing an expository sermon series, for example, pastors can find a healthy supply of informative commentaries, but there are few options for coming to terms with the overall teaching of each book of the New Testament. As well as being useful in sermon and Bible study preparation, the volumes will also be of value as textbooks in college and seminary exegesis classes. Our prayer is that they contribute to a deeper understanding of and commitment to the kingdom and glory of God in Christ.

The letter of James is one of the most practical in the New Testament, and believers often study it to learn what it means in everyday life to be a disciple of Jesus Christ. Some have raised questions about James—most famously Martin Luther—but the church has recognized the authority, power, and simplicity of what James wrote. We should remember, of course, that the letter is occasional. James doesn't pack all that he believed into five short chapters. The cross and resurrection of Jesus are not even mentioned, but that doesn't mean that James didn't believe in both of these. In fact, we know that he did, for we read in 1 Corinthians 15:1–11 that Jesus appeared to James after he was raised from the dead and that James and the rest of the apostles all believed and taught the gospel of the crucified and risen Lord (1 Cor. 15:11). In his letter, James centers on how believers express their new life, and Rob Plummer aptly titles his volume *Living Faith.* James reminds us that if our faith doesn't make a difference in the way we live, it is useless and, in fact, we don't have saving faith at all. In reading this book, you will be reminded of the vitality of the new life to which we are called and will be challenged to live a life of faith, hope, and love.

Thomas R. Schreiner and Brian S. Rosner

Abbreviations

BDAG	Danker, Frederick W., Walter Bauer, William F. Arndt, and F. Wilbur Gingrich, eds., *Greek-English Lexicon of the New Testament and Other Early Christian Literature.* 3rd ed. Chicago: University of Chicago Press, 2000.
BECNT	Baker Exegetical Commentary on the New Testament
BTNT	Biblical Theology of the New Testament
EGGNT	Exegetical Guide to the Greek New Testament
NICNT	The New International Commentary on the New Testament
NIGTC	The New International Greek Testament Commentary
NSBT	New Studies in Biblical Theology
BZNW	Beihefte zur Zeitschrift für die neutestamentliche Wissenschaft
PNTC	Pillar New Testament Commentary
SP	Sacra Pagina

Introduction

Author

THE AUTHOR OF THE EPISTLE OF JAMES describes himself simply as, "James, a servant of God and of the Lord Jesus Christ" (James 1:1). Although John Calvin suggested that perhaps James the son of Alphaeus (Matt. 10:3; Mark 3:18; Luke 6:15; Acts 1:13) wrote this letter, prior writers throughout church history are essentially unanimous in accepting James the son of Mary and half-brother of Jesus as the author.[1] While James was not a follower of Jesus during his earthly ministry (Mark 3:21; 6:3–4; John 7:3–5), Jesus appeared specially to him after his resurrection (1 Cor. 15:7), and thus James was considered an apostle (Gal. 1:19; 2:9). In the book of Acts, James takes a prominent role in the Jerusalem church, moderating the first "church council" and listing his name as the primary sender of a letter from the apostles and elders of the Jerusalem church (Acts 12:17; 15:13–29; 21:18–19).

In the Greek text, James's name is *Iakōbos*. Even if you don't know Greek, you can sound out the transliterated form of his name in the previous sentence. You will discover that the name is a Hellenized rendering of the Old Testament name "Jacob." Centuries-long transmission

1 His proposal can be found in John Calvin, *Commentaries on the Catholic Epistles*, trans. and ed. John Owen (repr.; Baker, 1999), 277. For extensive treatment of the authorship of the letter, see Dan G. McCartney, *James*, BECNT (Baker Academic, 2009), 8–32. McCartney observes, "Since the first explicit acknowledgement of the Epistle of James by Origen in the early third century, Christians have held that its author is James, known to Paul as 'the Lord's brother' " (McCartney, 14–15).

of the name through Latin, French, and finally into English affected its spelling and pronunciation, resulting in "James" in our modern English translations.[2] Readers should note that the adjective to describe something related to James or his epistle is "Jacobean," a word I use throughout this volume.

Date

According to historical records, James was killed in AD 62 by a mob fomented by Jewish religious authorities who were angry at his Christian influence on Jews in Jerusalem.[3] Thus, the letter of James must have been written prior to AD 62. Commentators have frequently noted features of the letter that one would expect from an early Palestinian setting—climatological references that fit the unique topography ("the early and the late rains," 5:7); assumptions of a Jewish-Christian audience's familiarity with the *Shema* ("you believe that God is one," 2:19); the labeling of an early Christian gathering as a "synagogue," *synagogē* ("a man . . . comes into your *assembly*," 2:2), rather than a "church," *ekklēsia*; and a close recapitulation of Jesus's teachings found in the Gospels (see chapter 1 below).

Genre

Although clearly written as a letter, the epistle of James lacks some of the typical features of letters we find in the New Testament and, for that matter, throughout the ancient world (e.g., a more specific identification of the addressees by name or location; a formulaic closing). The recipients of the letter are only identified as "the twelve tribes in the Dispersion" (1:1). It's not clear if we are to understand this language literally or symbolically. Perhaps James is writing to physical descendants of Abraham (i.e., people from the twelve tribes of ethnic Jews)

2 Although some popular writers have claimed that the spelling of the name "James" in English is due to King James I of England wanting his name to appear in the King James Version of the Bible, this claim is not accurate. Even in the 1526 Tyndale New Testament, the name of James is rendered as "Iames" ("James," with orthographic variation).

3 See Eusebius, *Ecclesiastical History* 2.23.18–19, where he quotes the account of Hegesippus; cf. Josephus, *Antiquities of the Jews* 20.9.1.

who are scattered outside the traditional land of Israel. Even if that is his intent, from James's subsequent statements in his letter, it is clear that such Jews are believers in Jesus, and thus they themselves would likely understand some level of eschatological and symbolic fulfillment in James's statement. As believers in Jesus, they are part of the true Israel that is circumcised in heart (Deut. 10:16; Jer. 4:4; 9:25–26; Rom. 2:29). Likely, they are scattered outside the traditional Holy Land (possibly because of persecution for their faith; cf. Acts 8:1), but they are also awaiting their true rest in the promised new heaven and new earth in the fulfillment of God's kingdom (Heb. 4:6–11; 11:39–40).

Organization

Scholars have offered many suggestions for the organization of the letter of James, including a comprehensive chiastic structure.[4] In light of the lack of agreement among learned commentators, it seems advisable to not be overly dogmatic. It's probably best just to recognize the clear discourse units that focus on particular theological or ethical motifs: for example, wicked speech (James 1:26; 3:1–12; 4:11–12), perseverance (1:2–4, 12; 5:7–11), prayer (1:5–8; 4:2–3; 5:13–18), living faith that produces works (1:22–25; 2:14–26), and the dangers of wealth (1:9–11; 2:1–7, 15–16; 5:1–6). In some ways, the letter of James is a like a pastoral blog—with a series of reflections about practical Christian living. It seems likely that James had knowledge about his addressees and the context in which they lived, but we can only approximate that knowledge through a cautious mirror-reading of his letter. For example, we know for certain that James taught against sinful favoritism (2:1–13); we do not know to what degree the recipients of his letter were engaging in favoritism or how much James knew of their behavior. We should be circumspect in reconstructing the setting of the letter beyond the explicit indicators James provides.

4 For a more extensive discussion of the structure of the letter of James, see McCartney, *James*, 58–67. He writes, "The difficulty of finding a convincing linear structure in James has resulted in a plethora of unconvincing or only partly convincing suggestions as to its organization and overall structure" (McCartney, 58).

In my treatment below of the prominent Jacobean themes, I have generally placed more dominant or pervasive theological themes earlier in the discussion. For example, James's Christological reflections underlie all his exhortation, so Christology is treated in chapter 1. The relationship of faith and works is one of the most prominent motifs in the letter and is thus treated in chapter 2. The ordering of chapters 3–7 seems a matter for less dogmatism, in my opinion.

1

Jesus Christ, the Lord of Glory

AT LEAST TWO BIBLICAL SCHOLARS have accused the epistle of James of being essentially a synagogue sermon with a couple of references to Jesus awkwardly inserted.[1] Nothing could be further from the truth. In fact, the letter of James is a faithful recapitulation of Jesus's teachings. In Matthew 7:24–25, Jesus said, "Everyone then who hears these words of mine and does them will be like a wise man who built his house on the rock. And the rain fell, and the floods came, and the winds blew and beat on that house, but it did not fall, because it had been founded on the rock." James's letter is an instruction manual about how to build one's life on the words of Jesus. In fact, one of the reasons that the letter of James is so popular for sermon series and group Bible studies is that genuine Christians are hungry to know how to live faithfully as Jesus's disciples.[2] The letter of James provides plenty of such instruction that is both clear and immediately applicable.

1 Louis Massebieau, "L'Épitre de Jacques est-elle l'oeuvre d'un chrétien?," *Revue de l'histoire des religions* 32 (1895): 249–83; Friedrich Spitta, "Der Brief des Jakobus," in *Zur Geschichte und Litteratur des Urchristentums* (Vandenhoeck & Ruprecht, 1896), 2:1–239. These works are cited and discussed by Martin Dibelius, *James: A Commentary on the Epistle of James*, rev. Heinrich Greeven, trans. Michael A. Williams, ed. Helmut Koester, Hermeneia (Fortress, 1975), 21–22.

2 A Christian publishing executive told me that commentaries and Bible studies on James are consistently top sellers.

Explicit References to Jesus

Unlike Paul's letters, the letter of James has few explicit references to the person of Jesus. As we explore the Christological nature of the letter, it seems advisable to start with the two passages where James unambiguously mentions Jesus by name.

In James 1:1, the author of the epistle identifies himself as "James, a servant of God and of the Lord Jesus Christ." Several things are noteworthy about James's reference. Jesus is identified with the title "Lord" (*kyrios*). Although "Lord" can be used as a title of polite address (similar to "sir" in modern English; see, e.g., John 4:11), the context of James 1:1 indicates that the author is using "Lord" as an exalted title. Jesus is a Lord whose followers are his slaves or servants, implying his authority and majesty in the spiritual realm. Furthermore, James calls himself one of these slaves/servants (i.e., a *doulos*) of this Lord, putting himself in both a place of submission and delegated representation. Because James was also a son of Mary, for him to identify himself as a slave/servant of his half brother was to recognize that Jesus was much more than a gifted rabbi (cf. 2 Cor. 5:16).

In James 1:1, Jesus is also called the Christ (*Christos*). *Christos* is a translation of the Hebrew word for "Messiah" and means "a person anointed" (by God). Scholars debate whether "Christ" always retains its titular sense in the New Testament or whether for some authors it almost functions like a second proper name of Jesus.[3] Regardless of one's conclusions about this question in other texts, it is unthinkable that the Jewish audience to which James wrote would not have understood a titular nuance to "Christ."

In the Old Testament, different classes of persons were anointed to set them apart for God-ordained tasks, most notably priests (Ex. 29:7), kings (1 Sam. 10:1), and prophets (1 Kings 19:16). Despite these anointings, Old Testament authors expected a preeminent anointed

3 L. W. Hurtado writes, "Close examination of *christos* in Paul's letters . . . shows that he uses the term almost as a name, or as part of the name for Jesus, and not characteristically as a title." L. W. Hurtado, "Christ," in *Dictionary of Jesus and the Gospels*, ed. Joel B. Green, Scot McKnight, and I. Howard Marshall (InterVarsity Press, 1992), 108.

one would eventually arrive (Isa. 42:1–4; Dan. 9:25)—an anointed one who would perfectly fulfill the priestly, kingly, and prophetic duties that forerunners had only anticipated and approximated. Jesus is that promised anointed one (Messiah/Christ); and in James's application of that title to Jesus, the apostle affirms the multifaceted biblical expectations for that role. To call Jesus both "Lord" and "Christ" in the opening lines of his letter is a clear affirmation of Jesus's authority, dominion, and messianic status.

James further instructs his readers in these opening lines by putting Jesus on a parallel plane with God, implying their equality and shared majesty. Both an equality of majesty and distinction of persons is communicated. James describes himself as a servant/slave of both the Lord Jesus Christ and of God. James does not employ the nuanced language of later creeds, but the way he speaks of God lays the groundwork for later Trinitarian reflection. God (the Father) is given equal glory alongside God the Son (Jesus), who is honored with the title *kyrios* (Lord), a term frequently used to translate the tetragrammaton (four-letter Hebrew name for God) in the Septuagint (e.g., Isa. 40:3). The Holy Spirit, the third person of the Trinity, is not mentioned here, but he is possibly appealed to later in the letter (James 4:5).[4]

James 2:1 includes the letter's only other explicit reference to Jesus by name. James writes, "My brothers, show no partiality as you hold the faith in our Lord Jesus Christ, the Lord of glory." Again, we see that

4 Douglas Moo offers this balanced analysis of James 4:5: "It is not clear whether James thinks of 'the spirit that he has made to dwell in us' as the Holy Spirit given to believers, or as God's creative spirit by which he has invigorated humankind (Gen. 2:7). Perhaps the latter is slightly more likely, however, since James never elsewhere refers to the Holy Spirit." Douglas J. Moo, *The Letter of James*, PNTC (Eerdmans, 2000), 190. Favoring a different interpretation, The NET Bible note on James 4:5 reads, "Interpreters debate the referent of the word 'spirit' in this verse: (1) The [NET] translation takes 'spirit' to be the lustful capacity within people that produces a divided mind (1:8, 14) and inward conflicts regarding God (4:1–4). God has allowed it to be in man since the fall, and he provides his grace (v. 6) and the new birth through the gospel message (1:18–25) to counteract its evil effects. (2) On the other hand, the word 'spirit' may be taken positively as the Holy Spirit and the sense would be, 'God yearns jealously for the Spirit he caused to live within us.' But the word for 'envious' or 'jealous' is generally negative in biblical usage and the context before and after seems to favor the negative interpretation."

Jesus is honored with the titles "Lord" and "Christ." Significantly, Jesus is further identified with the title "the Lord of glory." If there was any doubt about whether "Lord" had an exalted spiritual sense in application to Jesus, this appositional designation removes all such objections. Glory (i.e., the splendor of the divine presence) is something uniquely associated with God in the Scriptures and is only derivatively and partially experienced by God's people. We see, for example, in Revelation 7 the heavenly hosts ascribe glory (and other divine attributes) ultimately only to God:

> And all the angels were standing around the throne and around the elders and the four living creatures, and they fell on their faces before the throne and worshiped God, saying, "Amen! Blessing and *glory* and wisdom and thanksgiving and honor and power and might be to our God forever and ever! Amen." (Rev. 7:11–12)

Yes, humans hope in the glory they will experience in God's presence (Rom. 5:2) and are glorified by God (i.e., changed to reflect his glory, Rom. 8:30), but God alone is inherently glorious.

By calling Jesus "the Lord of glory," James ascribes to Jesus dominion over the realm of glory (i.e., the realm of God's splendor, perfection, goodness, and presence). Jesus himself is glorious and reigns as Lord over the realm of glory. Nevertheless, God the Son (Jesus) reigns in such a way that his lordship is never at odds with—and in fact only magnifies—the glory of the other members of the Trinity.

Debated References to Jesus

There are several other passages in the letter of James that contain the word "Lord" (*kyrios*) and could be understood as a reference to Jesus (1:7; 4:10, 15; 5:4, 7, 8, 10, 11, 14, 15). Some of these references to "Lord" have an immediate literary context that strongly favors God the Father as the referent for *kyrios*. For example, in James 1:7, James describes a person who prays doubtingly: "That person must not suppose that he will receive anything from the Lord." In the same discourse unit, James commands the person in need of wisdom to ask God (*theos*, 1:5). There can be little doubt that the referent for *kyrios* in 1:7 is God the Father who was just mentioned in 1:5. In other passages, there is arguably a bit of "Trinitarian ambiguity," which makes it more difficult to determine if James intended for his audience to understand the referent of *kyrios* as God the Father or God the Son. The situation is perhaps similar to many of the uses of the third person singular personal pronoun (*autos*) in the Johannine Epistles. About these pronouns, I. Howard Marshall astutely observes, "[John's] use of pronouns in this Epistle is sometimes vague."[5] Indeed, although the three persons of the triune God are distinct, when any one of those persons acts, the other members of the Trinity can rightly be spoken of as involved in the action. This is not modalism—equating the persons of the Trinity. The Father, the Son, and the Spirit are distinct—three persons, one divine Being. Systematic theologians have a term to describe this mutual indwelling of the members of the Trinity and the involvement of each member of the Trinity in the actions of every other member—that is, the doctrine of coinherence or perichoresis.

I encourage readers to open the letter of James and skim through the passages listed in the previous paragraph that contain the word "Lord" (1:7; 4:10, 15; 5:4, 7, 8, 10, 11, 14, 15). The majority of Christian commentators have detected contextual clues or stylized language mirroring the Old Testament to indicate that God the Father is the referent for most of the occurrences of *kyrios*.[6] For two of these additional passages, however, a strong case can be made that Jesus is in view.

In James 5:1–6, the apostle issues a strong condemnation of the wicked rich. As I will discuss later, this prophetic denunciation was likely intended to be overheard by the faithful addressees, serving both as a comfort in their suffering and as a warning not to be guilty of the same sins as their oppressors. Then, James goes on to encourage his Christian brothers and sisters: "Be patient, therefore, brothers, until the

5 I. Howard Marshall, *The Epistles of John*, NICNT (Eerdmans, 1978), 108n1.

6 E.g., Peter H. Davids, *The Epistle of James*, NIGTC (Eerdmans, 1982), 40–41.

coming of the *Lord*. See how the farmer waits for the precious fruit of the earth, being patient about it, until it receives the early and the late rains. You also, be patient. Establish your hearts, for the coming of the *Lord* is at hand" (5:7–8).

We find here two instances of Lord (italicized above). In light of so many early Christian communities awaiting the imminent second coming (*parousia*) of Jesus (Rom. 13:11–12; Phil. 4:5; 1 Thess. 4:16–17; Rev. 22:12), it seems likely that James's early readers would have understood "Lord" in James 5:7–8 as a reference to Jesus. Peter Davids agrees, observing,

> The majority of commentators note the strongly Christian tone throughout James, the doubtfulness of the references to the parousia of God, and the common technical sense of Parousia in the NT, and therefore argue that the event referred to is the coming of Christ. . . . This seems to be the most reasonable position.[7]

By calling Jesus "Lord" in 5:7–8, the apostle reminds us of the majesty and authority of Jesus. And by echoing Old Testament Scriptures that speak of the imminent day of the Lord (Isa. 13:6–9; Ezek. 30:2–3; Joel 2:1–2; Zeph. 1:14–15), James implies that Jesus will exercise divine authority to judge and rule when he comes. Conceptually, this passage in James 5:7–11 coheres with Paul's description of Christ's return in 2 Thessalonians 1:1–10. There, Paul assures the Thessalonians that God will

> grant relief to you who are afflicted as well as to us, when the Lord Jesus is revealed from heaven with his mighty angels in flaming fire, inflicting vengeance on those who do not know God and on those who do not obey the gospel of our Lord Jesus. They will suffer the punishment of eternal destruction, away from the presence of the Lord and from the glory of his might, when he comes on that day to

7 Davids, *The Epistle of James*, 182.

> be glorified in his saints, and to be marveled at among all who have believed, because our testimony to you was believed. (2 Thess. 1:7–10)

The other Jacobean uses of "Lord" with a strong likelihood of Jesus as the intended referent are found in James 5:14–15: "Is anyone among you sick? Let him call for the elders of the church, and let them pray over him, anointing him with oil in the name of the *Lord*. And the prayer of faith will save the one who is sick, and the *Lord* will raise him up. And if he has committed sins, he will be forgiven." Although there is ample Old Testament precedent for "the name of the LORD" to be a reference to Yahweh (Deut. 32:3; 1 Kings 8:17; Ps. 113:1–3; Prov. 18:10), in the New Testament we find a motif of Jesus's disciples acting and praying in his name (John 14:13–14; Acts 3:6; 4:10; Eph. 5:20; Col. 3:17). Furthermore, the only other text in the New Testament that speaks of anointing people for miraculous healing is when Jesus commissioned his disciples to go out and preach, heal, and cast out demons (Mark 6:13). In a passage that speaks of praying "in the name of the Lord" and promising that "the Lord will raise him up," early Christians would most naturally have understood the Lord Jesus as the referent for "Lord."

Parallels Between the Letter of James and the Teachings of Jesus

Nearly every verse in the letter of James could be laid alongside a teaching of Jesus from the Gospels to demonstrate that the epistle is a faithful, though selective, recapitulation of the Lord Jesus's instruction. Much of the letter parallels Jesus's teaching in the Sermon on the Mount, but prior to investigating that frequently observed pattern, let us consider teachings of Jesus and James on the new birth.

It is common in evangelical circles to emphasize the necessity of the new birth (conversion) as an essential element of true evangelical theology.[8] Indeed, one does not become a Christian by being born to

8 David W. Bebbington, *Evangelicalism in Modern Britain: A History form the 1730s to the 1980s* (Routledge, 1989), 1–19.

Christian parents. As Jesus tells Nicodemus, "Truly, truly, I say to you, unless one is born again he cannot see the kingdom of God" (John 3:3).

One might query, Isn't this teaching of Jesus a far cry from the epistle of James? Surely the letter of James is filled with moral injunctions and contains nothing about being born again, right? Absolutely not! In fact, the very same teaching about spiritual regeneration can be found clearly in James: "Of [God's] own will he brought us forth by the word of truth, that we should be a kind of firstfruits of his creatures" (James 1:18). Ultimately, why are some people Christians and other people not? James tells us that the decisive reason for this spiritual divide is the will of God: "*Of his own will* he brought us forth." The underlying Greek verb translated as "he brought us forth" (*apekyēsen*) usually refers to the physical act of giving birth, and many English translations choose to reflect this sense. For example, the NIV of James 1:18 reads, "He chose *to give us birth* through the word of truth, that we might be a kind of firstfruits of all he created."

What is the instrument that brings about this spiritual birth? It is "the word of truth." God's "word of truth" is his declared or written word that tells us the truth about who he is, who we are, and what he has done in Jesus to save us from our sins. As this saving word is heard, the Holy Spirit brings new life to elect sinners, formerly dead in their transgressions. They are born again! The apostle Paul similarly emphasizes the proclamation of the gospel as the means God uses to save sinners: "For 'everyone who calls on the name of the Lord will be saved.' How then will they call on him in whom they have not believed? And how are they to believe in him of whom they have never heard? And how are they to hear without someone preaching?" (Rom. 10:13–14, quoting Joel 2:32).

The people to whom James writes had heard the gospel (i.e., "the word of truth") and had experienced spiritual birth by the will of God. Furthermore, this new life, which they had received as a gift, was an anticipatory sign of the renewal of the entire cosmos that will happen when Jesus returns. In other words, Christians are "firstfruits"—the early part of the harvest dedicated to God that anticipates the final and complete harvest. We see, then, that a careful reading of James's letter coheres with both Jesus's teaching on the new birth and the apostle Paul's teaching about salvation.

Commentators have frequently noted the many parallels between the letter of James and the teachings of Jesus—especially in the Sermon on the Mount (Matt. 5–7). As these motifs in the epistle will be discussed in future chapters, perhaps it is best to see a brief summary and visual representation of some parallels at this point in the following table:

Table 1. Parallels between the letter of James and the teachings of Jesus

Topic	James	Jesus
Followers of Jesus are slaves	1:1	Luke 17:10
Rejoice in trials	1:2	Matt. 5:11–12
Perfection as the goal	1:3–4	Matt. 5:48
Be wise	1:5	Matt. 7:24–27; 10:16
God generously answers prayer	1:5	Matt. 7:7–8
Faith is essential	1:6–8	Matt. 9:29; 17:20
Blessed are the poor	1:9	Matt. 5:3; Luke 6:20
Woe to the rich	1:10–11; 5:1–6	Luke 6:24; 16:19–31
Endurance is required	1:12	Matt. 24:13
God is good	1:13, 17	Mark 10:18
Shun evil desires	1:14–15	Matt. 5:28–30
Be on guard against deception	1:16	Matt. 24:11
Spiritual birth from God	1:18	John 3:3–8
All creation will be renewed	1:18	Matt. 19:28
Be careful with words	1:19, 26	Matt. 12:36–37
Shun sinful anger	1:19–20	Matt. 5:22–26
Repent	1:21	Matt. 3:2; 4:17
The word grows in believers	1:21	Matt. 13:18–23
Be doers, not simply hearers	1:21–25	Matt. 7:21–27; 23:3
Jesus's teaching brings freedom	1:25	Luke 4:18; John 8:36
Care for the needy	1:27	Matt. 25:35–40; Luke 14:12–14
The glory of Jesus	2:1	Matt. 25:31

No favoritism toward the rich	2:1–13	Luke 14:12–14
Do not judge	2:4	Matt. 7:1
God's election of the unimpressive	2:5	Matt. 11:25
Love God	2:5	Matt. 22:37–38
Love your neighbor	2:8	Matt. 22:39
All God's law is binding	2:10–11	Matt. 5:17–20
Do not commit adultery	2:11	Matt. 5:27–30
Do not murder	2:11	Matt. 5:21–26
Imminent judgment	2:12	Matt. 24:42–44; 25:10–13
The measure you use shall be measured to you	2:13	Matt. 7:2
Words are not enough	2:14–26	Matt. 7:21–23
Deeds demonstrate identity	2:14–26	Matt. 7:15–20
The Lord is one	2:19	Mark 12:29
Demons perceive spiritual realities and tremble at them	2:19	Matt. 8:28–29; Mark 1:23–24; 3:11–12; Luke 8:28
Abraham as an example	2:21–24	Matt. 8:11; Luke 19:9; John 8:39–40
Rahab as an example	2:25–26	Matt. 1:5
Teachers held to a higher standard	3:1	Matt. 18:6, 23:1–35; Luke 12:47–48
Speech reveals identity	3:5–10	Matt. 15:10–11, 17–20
Gehenna—the place of final judgment	3:6	Matt. 5:22, 29–30; 10:28; 18:9; 23:15, 33
Be meek	3:13	Matt. 5:5
Be a peacemaker	3:17–18	Matt. 5:9
Spiritual identity shown by "fruit"	3:18	Matt. 7:15–20
External strife comes from inner corruption	4:1–2	Matt. 15:19–20
"Murder" of others	4:2	Matt. 5:21–26
"Adulterous" language to describe spiritual unfaithfulness	4:4	Matt. 12:39; 16:4
Loyalty to God vs. loyalty to "the world"	4:4	Mark 8:36–37; John 15:18–19; 17:14–16
Humble yourselves	4:6	Matt. 23:12
Need for pure hearts	4:8	Matt. 15:19–20

Do not judge	4:11–12	Matt. 7:1–5
Lifespan outside of human control	4:13–16	Matt. 6:27; Luke 12:20
Treasure on earth corruptible	5:3	Matt. 6:19
Wait attentively for the Lord's return	5:7–8	Matt. 24:36–51; 25:1–13
Do not grumble against fellow disciples	5:9	Matt. 18:15–17; Mark 9:33–35; Luke 22:24–27
Old Testament prophets as an example	5:10	Matt. 5:12; 23:29–36; Luke 6:22–23
Do not swear oaths	5:12	Matt. 5:33–37; 23:16–22
Pray in all circumstances	5:13–14	Luke 18:1–6
Christian leaders praying for the sick and anointing them with oil	5:14	Mark 6:13
Physical healing and spiritual forgiveness	5:15	Mark 2:1–12
Elijah as an example	5:17–18	Luke 4:25–26
Seek after the wandering brother	5:19–20	Matt. 18:10–20

Other Biblical Teaching on Salvation

James explicitly indicates that faith in the Lord Jesus and spiritual regeneration underlie all his moral instruction, though as modern readers of the letter, we are in danger of losing sight of that essential theological foundation if we dip into his correspondence haphazardly. Parallel to this pattern in the epistle of James, the Old Testament Scriptures are filled with moral instructions, but underlying those statutes are the story of God's gracious revelation of himself and his establishment of a relationship with his people through *his* saving work.

Moses declares to the Israelites in Deuteronomy 7:6–8,

> For you are a people holy to the LORD your God. The LORD your God has chosen you to be a people for his treasured possession, out of all the peoples who are on the face of the earth. It was not because you were more in number than any other people that the LORD set his love on you and chose you, for you were the fewest of all peoples, but it is because the LORD loves you and is keeping the oath that he swore to your fathers, that the LORD has brought you out with a

> mighty hand and redeemed you from the house of slavery, from the hand of Pharaoh king of Egypt.

Prior to the coming of the Messiah and his sacrificial death, God's people looked forward to the day when his chosen one would be "pierced for [their] transgressions" and "crushed for [their] iniquities" (Isa. 53:5). The blood of animals in their many sacrifices were a regular reminder of sin and the need for atonement, but as the author of Hebrews notes,

> For since the law has but a shadow of the good things to come instead of the true form of these realities, it can never, by the same sacrifices that are continually offered every year, make perfect those who draw near. Otherwise, would they not have ceased to be offered, since the worshipers, having once been cleansed, would no longer have any consciousness of sins? But in these sacrifices there is a reminder of sins every year. For it is impossible for the blood of bulls and goats to take away sins. (Heb. 10:1–4)

The ancient Israelites failed to obey God's holy laws and anticipated a day when God would institute a new covenant and write his law on their hearts (Jer. 31:31). They knew a day was coming when God would remove the sin of the land in a single day (Zech. 3:8–9). Yet, like the book of James, this soteriological foundation of Old Testament teaching is not always on the surface of every biblical text.

Jesus provided much practical ethical instruction, but such teaching must likewise be understood in relation to the Lord's claims about himself and his role in God's saving plan. Jesus said, "I am the way, and the truth, and the life. No one comes to the Father except through me" (John 14:6). Elsewhere he said, "The Son of Man came to seek and to save the lost" (Luke 19:10). The apostle John instructs us that unless we trust in Jesus's propitiatory death, the righteous wrath of God remains on us: "Whoever believes in the Son has eternal life; whoever does not obey the Son shall not see life, but the wrath of God remains on him"

(John 3:36; cf. 1 John 2:2). Similar to the way we read the letter of James, we need to remember that Jesus's instructions about how his followers should live assume that his disciples have first recognized their need of his forgiveness (Luke 18:9–14), bowed the knee under his lordship (Matt. 16:24), and received the empowerment of his Spirit (Acts 1:8). Salvation is a free and undeserved gift, but the free gift of salvation initiates one as a loyal subject of God's kingdom.

Conclusion

When Jesus walked along the Emmaus road with two unnamed disciples, Luke tells us that Jesus rebuked them:

> And he said to them, "O foolish ones, and slow of heart to believe all that the prophets have spoken! Was it not necessary that the Christ should suffer these things and enter into his glory?" And beginning with Moses and all the Prophets, he interpreted to them in all the Scriptures the things concerning himself. (Luke 24:25–27)

If the Old Testament is all about Jesus (and it is), then how much more is the New Testament focused on Christ! The letter of James is no exception. Admittedly, the letter has only two explicit references to Jesus by name (1:1; 2:1), but the whole letter pulsates with the teaching of Jesus—sometimes in nearly word-for-word quotations (e.g., Matt. 5:34–37; James 5:12). More commonly, the teaching of Jesus is selectively reported and slightly repackaged for a new generation of disciples seeking to be faithful to their Lord.

2

Living Faith That Has Works

MANY CHRISTIANS HAVE HEARD that the Reformer Martin Luther was critical of the epistle of James. In fact, Luther once said, "The epistle of James is a right strawy epistle in comparison with them [i.e., John, Romans, Galatians, Ephesians, and 1 Peter], since indeed it has no evangelical nature to it."[1] Elsewhere, Luther provocatively wrote,

> Many have mightily labored to reconcile James with Paul, just as Philip (Melanchthon) has done in the Apology (to the Augsburg Confession), but not with real success. These are at odds: faith justifies, faith does not justify. If there is anyone who can bring these into harmony with one another, I will set my [doctoral] biretta on him, and let him scold me as a fool.[2]

Luther was right to see an emphasis on faith and works in the letter of James, but the contrast is not between faith and works. Rather, James distinguishes between a living faith (that produces works) and a dead

1 This comment comes from Luther's general introduction to the "Septembertestament" (published on September 21, 1522) in Martin Luther, *Luthers Werke: Kritische Gesamtausgabe [Briefwechsel]*, 73 vols. (Hermann Böhlau, 1883–2009), 6.10. Cited in Timo Laato, "Justification According to James: A Comparison with Paul," *Trinity Journal* 18, no. 1 (1997): 43. The article was translated for *Trinity Journal* by Mark A. Seifrid.

2 Martin Luther, *Luthers Werke: Kritische Gesamtausgabe [Tischreden]*, 3.253:3292a, as cited in Laato, "Justification According to James," 44.

faith (that has no works). Arguably, the main theme of James's letter is on the necessity of true believers to have a living faith—one that evidences itself with observable acts of obedience and love. This is the picture of a genuine, mature, wholly formed follower of Jesus.

In this chapter, we will explore the topic of faith and works by examining three foundational concepts for James—dead faith, repentance, and living faith. First, we will look at the category of dead or defective faith, which "does not have works" (James 2:17). In invoking this category, James warns his recipients against hypocrisy and divinely condemned empty religiosity. Next, we will look at the necessity of repentance from dead or defective faith. Third, we will survey the category of living faith, which *has* works.

Because of James's use of terms like "perfect" (*teleios*, 1:4, 17, 25; 3:2) and "wise/wisdom" (*sophos/sophia*, 1:5; 3:13, 15, 17) to describe mature believers, I will also briefly discuss these two categories—perfection and wisdom. Finally, I will demonstrate that James's teaching on faith and works accords with the Old Testament, Jesus's teachings, and the remainder of the New Testament.

Dead Faith

James is a realist about religion. He frequently invokes the category of dead, deficient, or false faith as a foil to the living faith that the apostle enjoins on his readers. Indeed, James repeatedly warns his readers that verbal claims or religious self-assessments do not necessarily indicate one's true spiritual condition. To properly understand the category of living faith, one must also acknowledge the category of dead faith. One category necessitates the other.

James wastes no time in introducing the category of defective faith. In James 1:5, he commands persons who lack wisdom to ask God for it. The apostle further notes that some persons who petition God for wisdom may not really ask "in faith" (1:6). In other words, they ask God but doubt whether he is good, able, or inclined to answer their petitions. James tells us, "That person must not suppose that he will receive anything from the Lord; he is a double-minded man, unstable in all his ways" (1:7–8). James does not construct a nuanced continuum but only offers two ways of prayer—one in faith and one doubting. And the doubting man is double minded and receives nothing. We should observe that the doubting, double-minded man still has an outward religious expression—in this case, prayer for wisdom. Yet, that outward religiosity is condemned as tragically deficient.

James's exhortation about praying in faith is reflective of much of his letter. James confronts his readers with stark spiritual dichotomies, similar to patterns found in wisdom literature, such as the book of Proverbs or in the opening lines of the Didache.[3] James's polarities confront the reader with the realization that, in the final analysis, beliefs and behaviors only end in one of two ways—life or death. With such a confrontation comes the invitation to respond appropriately.

Christians with sensitive consciences may feel too easily condemned by James's insistence that prayer be offered in faith. Indeed, for a modern reader to summarily tell other persons that they have not had their prayers answered because they do not have the requisite faith would likely be spiritual abuse. Yet, in constructing a full-orbed biblical view on faith, we must remember that Jesus repeatedly demands faith from those who approach him and qualifies his healings with statements such as "According to your faith be it done to you" (Matt. 9:29). When Jesus's disciples could not heal a child with demonically induced seizures, they privately asked Jesus why. He replied "Because of your little faith. For truly, I say to you, if you have faith like a grain of mustard seed, you will say to this mountain, 'Move from here to there,' and it will move, and nothing will be impossible for you" (Matt. 17:20).

In noting the necessity of faith in prayer, however, James does not condemn the maturing cry of a striving faith ("I believe; help my unbelief!" Mark 9:24); he is instead describing the mindset of one who

3 The Didache 1:1–2 reads, "There are two ways, one of life and one of death, and there is a great difference between these two ways. Now this is the way of life: First, you shall love God, who made you. Second, you shall love your neighbor as yourself; but whatever you do not wish to happen to you, do not do to another." *The Apostolic Fathers: Greek Texts and English Translations*, 3rd ed., ed. and trans. Michael W. Holmes (Baker Academic, 2007), 345.

does not rely on God while emptily mouthing a petition for help. Praying while not trusting the goodness, power, or inclination of God fits in the category of deficient faith, hypocrisy, and empty religiosity. At the same time, it cannot be emphasized enough that to insist on faith for answered prayer is not the same as concluding that unanswered prayer is *necessarily* a sign of defective faith.

James's statement about a lack of faith resulting in unanswered prayer is analogous to his later comment that a sickness *might* result from sin and, thus, that confession of sin *could* be appropriate for the sick person (James 5:15–16). The Bible's teaching on sickness and sin is quite nuanced and will not fit into the reductionistic schemes one frequently encounters in popular religion. Sickness may result from sin (1 Cor. 11:30). Sickness and even death may be fatherly discipline—or even judgment—from God (Acts 5:1–11; 1 Cor. 11:29–32). More commonly, it would seem, a person's sickness or disability has no correlation with sin, and yet, sickness is not outside God's sovereign purposes of bringing glory to his name (John 9:3).

A superficial hearing of God's word is also an example of defective faith. James avers that a person is self-deceived if he only listens to the word of God but does not alter his behavior in response to that word (James 1:22). He explains, "For if anyone is a hearer of the word and not a doer, he is like a man who looks intently at his natural face in a mirror. For he looks at himself and goes away and at once forgets what he was like" (1:23–24). The key purpose of this analogy is to condemn superficial knowledge accompanied by lack of action. The world is filled with religious pretenders, and James repeatedly warns his recipients against the dire situation of being found in that category,

Sinful speech is another sign of insincere or inauthentic faith. James writes, "If anyone thinks he is religious and does not bridle his tongue but deceives his heart, this person's religion is worthless" (James 1:26). To "bridle the tongue" is a broad category that encompasses the idea of guarding one's speech from all manner of sinful utterance, such as slander, lies, or coarse jesting (cf. Ex. 20:16; Lev. 19:16; Prov. 6:16–19; 12:22; 26:18–19). Speech is an overflow of the heart (Luke 6:45), and sinful patterns of speech indicate the true nature of one's faith. To have a life characterized by sinful speech and still think oneself "spiritual" or "religious" is to be self-deceived, declares James. Over time, both our words and our actions show who we really are (Matt. 7:15–20).

James further observes that a life exhibiting sinful favoritism is inconsistent with a healthy, living faith in the Lord Jesus. Only a dead, deceptive, or inconsistent faith is characterized by sinful favoritism. James commands, "My brothers, show no partiality as you hold the faith in our Lord Jesus Christ, the Lord of glory" (James 2:1). Literally, the text translates as "My brothers, do not hold in favoritisms the faith of our Lord Jesus Christ of glory." Even as James lays out such polarizing theological appeals, he reminds his readers that he is their spiritual sibling, and by calling them "brothers," he assures them that he is appealing to them as a fellow community member. James's imperative not to "have" or "hold" (*echō*) the faith in "favoritisms" (or "acts of favoritism") is unusual. Rather than using the verb for believe (*pisteuō*), James chooses the expression "have faith in" or "hold faith in." Perhaps this word choice serves to highlight the motif of objectively demonstrable faith—whether as a living or dead reality—that we find throughout James's letter. The dative plural "favoritisms" (*prosōpolēmpsiais*) implies that a faith marred by sinful partiality will have varied manifestations of that favoritism. The genitive "of glory" (*tēs doxēs*), qualifying the implied repetition of the noun "Lord" (*kyrios*), instructs the readers that there is, indeed, one person who is worthy of special honor and preferential treatment—Jesus Christ, the Lord of glory. If we rightly honor Jesus as glorious, how then can we mistreat his image bearers and fawn over some people for our selfish benefit? To treat someone preferentially within the Christian community because she is rich or socially connected or beautiful or famous is to adopt the world's values and to deny the faith one professes. A living, healthy faith in the glorious Lord Jesus Christ will not express itself in opportunistic obsequiousness.

In James 2:14–26, the apostle homes in on a prime example of dead faith. He describes a member of the Christian community who sees a Christian brother or sister in need, presumably has the ability to help him or her, but fails to provide any tangible assistance. James declares, “So also faith by itself, if it does not have works, is dead” (2:17). Thus, James instructs us that there are two categories of faith—(1) faith that *has* works and is thus living and (2) faith that does *not have* works and is thus dead. Works and faith are not the same thing. Rather, works are produced by a genuine faith and are, therefore, evidence of it. In fact, James’s explicit language would even call into question my use above of the verb “produced.” Genuine faith *has* works. Works are inherent and organic to living, saving faith.

Simply to affirm monotheism (“God is one,” 2:19) is not sufficient to prove one has a living faith. Even the demons believe (intellectually) that there is one God and tremble in response—a response that, ironically, is more visible and measurable than the reaction one expects from a person of dead faith. Intellectual or propositional statements about God, while necessary and proper, are inadequate to discern if one has a living or dead faith. James provides this pungent summary: “For as the body apart from the spirit is dead, so also faith apart from works is dead” (2:26).

We will return to James 2:14–26 below in the discussion of living faith. Before those reflections, however, we need to survey James’s teaching on the necessity of repentance.

Repentance

Alongside the warning against a false, defective, or dead faith comes the concomitant appeal to turn from that dead faith. The letter of James has more imperatives per total word count than any other New Testament book;[4] and each imperative can be understood, in some sense, as an appeal to turn from defective faith to a healthy faith. A Christian experiences initial repentance when he turns from spiritual deadness to the gospel and is reconciled to God (Acts 2:37–38). Subsequently, Christians living as sons and daughters of God experience daily acts of repentance as they turn from thoughts and actions that do not align

4 William Varner, *James: A Commentary on the Greek Text* (Fontes, 2017), 21–22.

with their new spiritual identity. Jesus taught the necessary pattern of such daily repentance via the Lord's Prayer by instructing his disciples that the model of daily prayer includes this petition:

> Forgive us our debts,
> as we also have forgiven our debtors. (Matt. 6:12)

Some readers have been surprised by the ending of James's letter. It says, "My brothers, if anyone among you wanders from the truth and someone brings him back, let him know that whoever brings back a sinner from his wandering will save his soul from death and will cover a multitude of sins" (James 5:19–20).

This final passage reminds us that the entire letter is a call to repentance. Each exhortation, each truth, each spiritual reality erects a holy standard alongside the reader or persons in the reader's sphere of influence. In these concluding words, James envisions the attentive reader seeking after a straying sheep and, empowered by the Spirit, calling such a wandering one to repentance and renewed faith.

Though the basic meaning of this final section of James's letter is quite clear, some of the language is unexpected. James does not say that turning another member of the Christian community from sin will bring him to a place of greater fruitfulness or blessing. He says turning the wandering person will "save his soul from death" (5:20). At this point, we should look back to 5:19 and note that this person has "wander[ed] from the truth"—a serious description of spiritual desertion. In other words, from all outward appearances, this person has abandoned the Christian community, and his embrace of sin is so public and potentially disqualifying that for him to continue in rebellion is to call into question his salvation. From all outward observations, he is running down the road toward eternal ruin and spiritual death. Nevertheless, James says, God can use you, Christian reader, as an instrument to turn the wandering sinner back to the path of life. Indeed, the passionate and concerned involvement of Christians in one another's lives is one of the means that God employs to preserve his people.[5] In other words, concerned Christians are one of the instruments God uses to bring about his promise of preserving his people from ultimate spiritual ruin. A true Christian may wander or stray, but God will bring him back, and what joy we have if God uses us to seek out and bring back a lost sheep (cf. Matt. 18:13–14; Luke 15:7)! We delight to see a Christian's repentance from a multitude of sins that pulled him down the road to death.

As we read through the varied commands, we must remember that James expects his readers to be challenged by his letter. He wants these Christian brothers and sisters to have lives of greater faithfulness and obedience. While the sovereignty of God is consistently maintained in James's epistle, there is no less emphasis on the necessity of humans to respond rightly to God's revelation of himself. Where our lives do not reflect God's holy standards, we are called to repentance. And, for Christians reading James's letter, this repentance is not part of the initial formation of a relationship but the experience of fatherly forgiveness in the context of ongoing spiritual sonship.

Living Faith

The standard of a living faith underlies virtually all the instruction in the letter, but James 1:21–27 provides a helpful overview of some of the foundational issues associated with this motif. We read, "Therefore put away all filthiness and rampant wickedness and receive with meekness the implanted word, which is able to save your souls" (1:21). The word "therefore" (*dio*) looks back to the previous verse in which James states that human anger "does not produce the righteousness of God" (1:20). In light of *that* fact—that sinful human anger does not produce righteous behavior that is pleasing to God—James calls on the letter's recipients to repent from "all filthiness and rampant wickedness." He calls them to leave behind

5 See Thomas R. Schreiner and Ardel B. Caneday, *The Race Set Before Us: A Biblical Theology of Perseverance and Assurance* (IVP Academic, 2001).

behavior that does not accord with God's character—he calls them to repent (see above).

A living faith, however, does not just turn away from sin but toward God. James commands, "Receive with meekness the implanted word, which is able to save your souls" (James 1:21). This command to "receive with meekness the implanted word" corresponds to Jesus's injunction to "believe in the gospel" in Mark 1:15. To turn away from something is to turn toward something else. Biblically, to repent is not only to turn away from sin but also to turn toward God's good revelation of himself—his promises and his truth.

James's language is unexpected. How can one "receive" something that is already "implanted"? The phrase "implanted word" calls to mind Jesus's parable of the sower (Matt. 13:1–23; Mark 4:1–20; Luke 8:4–15), in which the dispersed seed represents the word of God (Mark 4:14). Depending on the type of soil (i.e., hearts) that the seed lands in, it can take root and produce an abundant crop or be choked out by worries and cares of this life. James calls on his addressees to nurture the implanted word, letting it grow and influence their values, thoughts, and actions. He charges them, "But be doers of the word, and not hearers only, deceiving yourselves" (James 1:22). Here then is the *sine qua non* of living faith—doing the word.

Arguably, the epicenter of James's discussion of living faith is found in 2:14–16. James queries, "What good is it, my brothers, if someone says he has faith but does not have works? Can that faith save him?" (2:14). We note again that James addresses the recipients of his letter as "brothers" (*adelphoi*). Although James includes much strongly worded and confrontational teaching, his instruction comes in the context of a committed spiritual family.

Note carefully the wording of 2:14. James addresses a person who *says* (*legō*) that he has faith. James does *not* report that the person has faith but, rather, that the person *says* that he has faith. Furthermore, note the ESV's apt rendering of the anaphoric Greek article here (*hē*)—"Can *that* faith save him?" James is not dismissing faith in and of itself; he is dismissing the spurious claim to faith. Indeed, the faith this hypothetical person actually has is false, inadequate, and dead because it is a type of faith that does not have works (2:17, 20).

Later, James highlights the important category of visual expression. He writes, "But someone will say, 'You have faith and I have works.' Show me your faith apart from your works, and I will show you my faith by my works" (2:18). The rhetorical opponent proposes that faith and works are separable gifts—that it is possible to have one without the other ("You have faith and I have works"). James disagrees and says that true faith is inseparable from works; a living faith has/contains works. James repeats the verb "show" (*deiknumi*) to highlight that the reality of one's faith only becomes visible through one's deeds (2:18; cf. 3:13).

James further develops the category of visible demonstration/proof when he discusses Abraham's obedient offering of Isaac in response to God's command. He writes, "You *see* that faith was active along with [Abraham's] works, and faith was completed by his works" (2:22). The prevalence and prominence of vocabulary communicating visual display ("show," 2:18 [2x]; "see," 2:22, 24) lead us to conclude that the verb *dikaioō* in 2:21 is probably better translated with the nuance of "show to be in the right" rather than "justified" (contra the ESV). The NLT captures the sense nicely: "Don't you remember that our ancestor Abraham *was shown to be right* (*edkiaiōthē*) with God by his actions when he offered his son Isaac on the altar?" (2:21). Even the Catholic Jacobean scholar Patrick Hartin, whom one might expect to be biased toward finding the doctrine of justification by works in this passage, concludes that "show/demonstrate as righteous" is the proper translation of *dikaioō* in 2:21. Hartin writes, "In James the concern is very different [than Paul]. Works (that is, good deeds) show that one's faith is living and that one is in a right relationship with God. Hence, *dikaioun* [i.e., the verb *dikaioō*] in the context of James bears the meaning 'demonstrates righteousness.' "[6]

6 Patrick J. Hartin, *James*, SP 14 (Liturgical, 2003), 153–54.

Perfection

In the letter of James, every good and "perfect" (*teleios*) gift is affirmed as having come from God (1:17). God's inscripturated revelation fulfilled in Christ is described as "the perfect [*teleios*] law, the law of liberty" (1:25). Such perfection also finds expression in the lives of mature believers who reflect God's character so consistently that they are described with the following attributes: "perfect" (*teleioi/teleios*, 1:4; 3:2), "complete" (*holoklēroi*, 1:4), "lacking in nothing" (*en mēdeni leipomenoi*, 1:4), "completed" (*eteleiōthē*, 2:22). Considered in isolation, these stark descriptors might lead a reader to conclude that, according to James, actual perfect (i.e., sinless) behavior is attainable for the mature Christian in this life. Yet, it is necessary to read these descriptors alongside other statements of James, such as "We all stumble in many ways" (3:2). In fact, James does not teach a doctrine of perfectionism.[7] He employs somewhat hyperbolic language to emphasize the radical transformation that God's presence brings to the lives of believers. Furthermore, he proleptically declares the perfection that will, indeed, be every believer's inheritance in Christ (cf. 1 Cor. 2:9; 13:12).

Numerous scholars have recognized that James is not alone in applying the language of "perfection" or "completeness" to describe a comparative spiritual maturity that is outwardly recognizable. In his book *A Spirituality of Perfection: Faith in Action in the Letter of James*, Patrick Hartin observes,

> The notion of integrity expresses well the [Jacobean] concept of perfection. Integrity demands consistency in word and action. This integrity is both personal and communitarian. The values that influence the lives of both the individual and the community are distinct from the world. In fact, believers should be a sign to the world of the consistency between their faith and their action. This harmony

7 See Andrew David Naselli, *Let Go and Let God? A Survey and Analysis of Keswick Theology* (Lexham, 2010).

is the hallmark of James's message. James gives a very positive assessment of works (not "works of the law" in the sense that Paul attacks). James's focus on works centers on deeds of mercy that entail a constant concern for the needs and welfare of others, be it orphans and widows (1:27), the poor, or those discriminated against (2:1–7). Christian integrity demands a social conscience and response. James envisages that his readers (including present-day readers) demonstrate they are people of integrity.[8]

Wisdom

Although an epistle, the letter of James has undeniable similarities to wisdom literature.[9] Wisdom literature is a recognized genre of ancient Near Eastern literature that focuses on the practicalities of a life well lived. In the Bible, such a life begins with a reverence for and submission to God (Prov. 9:10). James addresses many of the same themes found in wisdom literature: integrity of speech (James 1:19, 26; 3:1–10; 4:11–12), wealth and poverty (1:9–11, 27; 2:1–7, 14–17; 4:13–17; 5:1–6), the dangers of hypocrisy and disobedience (1:22–26; 2:14–20; 3:9–12; 4:17; 5:12), and so on. In James 3:13–18, the terminology of "wisdom" comes to the surface of the text:

> Who is wise and understanding among you? By his good conduct let him show his works in the meekness of wisdom. But if you have bitter jealousy and selfish ambition in your hearts, do not boast and be false to the truth. This is not the wisdom that comes down from above, but is earthly, unspiritual, demonic. For where jealousy and selfish ambition exist, there will be disorder and every vile practice. But the wisdom from above is first pure, then peaceable, gentle, open to reason, full of mercy and good fruits, impartial and sincere. And a harvest of righteousness is sown in peace by those who make peace.

8 Patrick J. Hartin, *A Spirituality of Perfection: Faith in Action in the Letter of James* (Liturgical, 1999), 155.

9 The sapiential contours of James are frequently noted in Varner, *James*, 25–26.

Although the entire letter of James addresses the common topics of wisdom literature (in epistolary form, of course), in this short text (James 3:13–17) we find wisdom words (*soph-*) repeated four times (3:13 [2x], 15, 17). As in the book of Proverbs or more broadly in ancient Near Eastern wisdom literature, we find that the meaning of wisdom is assumed more than defined. Rather, the emphasis is on the characteristics, attitudes, and behaviors of a person living a wise life. James tells us that a wise person is not motivated by selfishness or bitter jealousy (3:15). Instead, rooted in purity, humility, impartiality, and sincerity, the truly wise person shows his wisdom by his righteous and peaceable conduct (3:17–18). Although employing different terminology, James's reflections on wisdom accord with his statements about genuine faith that has works (2:14–26). Genuinely wise people also have visible works that testify to the reality of their wisdom (3:13–18).

In his discourse analysis of the letter of James, William Varner concludes that James 3:13–18 is the "thematic peak" of the letter. Varner observes how all new topics are introduced throughout the letter of James with the repeated vocative "my brothers" (*adelphoi mou*). The exceptions to this are two rhetorical questions, one of which introduces the "thematic peak" of the letter (3:13) and the other introduces the "hortatory peak" of the letter (4:1). Varner writes,

> The two topics introduced, not by "brothers" but by a rhetorical question, serve as the two peaks (thematic and hortatory) that convey the main themes of the letter in the prominent way. The task of the student/teacher/preacher of James is to discern how each paragraph develops its topic along the lines of the behavior condemned (which follows earthly wisdom) and the behavior commended (which follows heavenly wisdom). The task is to recognize that wholeness, completeness, maturity, and their consequent peace (3:18) will be the result of his hearers and readers making the wise choice of heavenly wisdom.[10]

10 Varner, *James*, 38.

Wisdom is undoubtedly a topic on which James expounds. Furthermore, the concept of wisdom arguably underlies (or at least accords with) much of James's teaching. Yet, we must also admit that wisdom words (*soph-*) do not occur with enough frequency that we could call wisdom a prominent motif in the letter. Though helpful and thought provoking in his study, Varner likely claims too much for James 3:13–18.

Other Biblical Teaching on Faith and Works

James frequently quotes from or alludes to the Old Testament Scriptures (e.g., 1:11; 2:8, 23; 4:6; 5:11, 17–18). The apostle unambiguously presents his letter as in harmony with both the Old Testament and the teachings of Jesus. It is no surprise, then, that James's teaching on faith and works agrees with instructions on faith and works scattered throughout the Old Testament and in the Gospels.

In Genesis 3, we see that the foundational divine demand of humans is faith. God gives Adam and Eve guidelines for living in paradise. Their proper response to his gracious instructions should be faith/trust and, consequently, obedience. In other words, the first humans should have trusted God's warning not to eat from the tree of the knowledge of good and evil, and such trust should have resulted in obedience. Instead, the humans doubted God and disobeyed (Gen. 3:6). Tragically, a lack of faith and subsequent disobedience resulted in the fall of the entire creation into decay and disorder (Gen. 3:16–19; Rom. 8:19–22).

In this broken world, the fundamental demand God continues to make on humanity is faith—that we take him at his revealed word. Indeed, "whoever would draw near to God must believe that he exists and that he rewards those who seek him" (Heb. 11:6). Abraham embodied the proper response to God. When the Lord declared to the patriarch that his offspring would be as numerous as the stars in the sky, Abraham "believed the Lord, and he counted it to him as righteousness" (Gen. 15:5–6). Abraham further responded in faith to God's instructions by obediently taking Isaac to Mount Moriah to sacrifice him (Gen. 22:1–18). In this account, we observe obedience as an evidence and fruit of faith (James 2:21–23).

Throughout Israel's history there were many examples of false or superficial faith that God called out as religious hypocrisy. In the day of Amos, God expressed his disgust at religiosity that was not a true response to his revealed word. As reported by Amos, God declared to the hypocrites in Israel,

> I hate, I despise your feasts,
> and I take no delight in your solemn assemblies.
> Even though you offer me your burnt offerings and grain offerings,
> I will not accept them;
> and the peace offerings of your fattened animals,
> I will not look upon them.
> Take away from me the noise of your songs;
> to the melody of your harps I will not listen.
> But let justice roll down like waters,
> and righteousness like an ever-flowing stream. (Amos 5:21–24)

The Israelites should have cared for the poor and worked for justice. Instead, they exploited the poor and leveraged the religious and social systems for their self-aggrandizement (Amos 2:6–7; 4:11; 5:11–12).

Throughout God's prior revelation in the Old Testament, we find repeated calls for sinners to turn from their rebellion and back to God. Sometimes the repentance is individualistic, as in the case of David when he sinned by committing adultery with Bathsheba and killing her husband, Uriah (2 Sam. 12:1–15). After being confronted by the prophet Nathan, David responded, "I have sinned against the Lord" (2 Sam. 12:13), acknowledging his personal guilt and realigning himself with the revealed will of God.

Other times in the Old Testament, we see a corporate dimension to repentance, as when Ezekiel declares this oracle of God to the rebellious chosen nation: "Therefore I will judge you, O house of Israel, every one according to his ways, declares the Lord God. Repent and turn from all your transgressions, lest iniquity be your ruin" (Ezek. 18:30). A foundational sign of a living faith is repentance, a turning away from sin.

In the Old Testament, we also find the anticipation of a future day in which God will do a new work among his covenant people. God will bring about an internalization of his word, such that living faith and visible obedience will testify to the spiritual surgery he has done on his people's hearts. Jeremiah 31:31–34 is one of several paradigmatic texts (cf. Ezek 36:22–38) that speak of this day, which was fulfilled in the life and ministry of Jesus:

> Behold, the days are coming, declares the LORD, when I will make a new covenant with the house of Israel and the house of Judah, not like the covenant that I made with their fathers on the day when I took them by the hand to bring them out of the land of Egypt, my covenant that they broke, though I was their husband, declares the LORD. For this is the covenant that I will make with the house of Israel after those days, declares the LORD: I will put my law within them, and I will write it on their hearts. And I will be their God, and they shall be my people. And no longer shall each one teach his neighbor and each his brother, saying, "Know the LORD," for they shall all know me, from the least of them to the greatest, declares the LORD. For I will forgive their iniquity, and I will remember their sin no more.

Finally, in holding the Old Testament up alongside the letter of James, we note a repeated call for God's people to aim at perfection/wholeness/maturity (Gen. 17:1; Deut. 18:13; 1 Kings 8:61; Pss. 15:1–2; 119:1) and to be wise (Deut. 4:6; Job 28:28; Ps. 90:12; Prov. 1:7; 3:13–18; 4:7; Eccl. 7:12).

The living faith enjoined by the letter of James finds much similarity with Jesus's teaching. Jesus repeatedly condemned religious hypocrisy, called for repentance, and demanded that people place their faith in him and subsequently live in obedience to his lordship. Matthew 23 is probably one of the best-known extended condemnations of dead faith or religious hypocrisy. Among many other strong words, Jesus said, "Woe to you, scribes and Pharisees, hypocrites! For you clean the outside of the cup and the plate, but inside they are full of greed and self-indulgence" (Matt. 23:25). Immediately following this condemnation of religious hypocrisy is a call to repentance: "You blind Pharisee! First clean the inside of the cup and the plate, that the outside also may be clean" (Matt. 23:26). Dead, inadequate, or false faith can only be remedied by repentance.

Though Jesus's particularism offends modern pluralistic sensibilities, he unambiguously taught that the destiny of every person turns on his or her reaction to him:

> On the last day of the feast, the great day, Jesus stood up and cried out, "If anyone thirsts, let him come to me and drink. Whoever believes in me, as the Scripture has said, 'Out of his heart will flow rivers of living water.'" Now this he said about the Spirit, whom those who believed in him were to receive, for as yet the Spirit had not been given, because Jesus was not yet glorified. (John 7:37–39)

Jesus demanded repentance and unqualified trust in him. The Gospel of Mark offers this definitive summary of Jesus's proclamation: "The time is fulfilled, and the kingdom of God is at hand; repent and believe in the gospel" (Mark 1:15).

Just like James, Jesus taught that behavior reveals identity. Both false and genuine faith—true and genuine spirituality/religion—are shown through actions. Jesus declared,

> Beware of false prophets, who come to you in sheep's clothing but inwardly are ravenous wolves. You will recognize them by their fruits. Are grapes gathered from thornbushes, or figs from thistles? So, every healthy tree bears good fruit, but the diseased tree bears bad fruit. A healthy tree cannot bear bad fruit, nor can a diseased tree bear good fruit. Every tree that does not bear good fruit is cut down and thrown into the fire. Thus you will recognize them by their fruits.
>
> Not everyone who says to me, "Lord, Lord," will enter the kingdom of heaven, but the one who does the will of my Father who is in heaven. (Matt. 7:15–21)

Finally, Jesus taught that his disciples should be "perfect" (*teleioi*), as their heavenly Father is perfect (Matt. 5:48). And Jesus instructed his disciples to be wise ("wise as serpents and innocent as doves," Matt. 10:16), just as James instructed the recipients of his letter to strive for perfection (James 1:4; 3:2) and to be wise (3:13–18). This call for maturity/perfection is echoed elsewhere in the New Testament (Rom. 12:2; Col. 1:28; Heb. 6:1).

Conclusion

Perhaps the dominant theme of James's letter is the necessity of true Christians to have a living faith that evidences itself in obedience. Dead or defective faith is condemned (James 2:14–17); wandering Christians should be called to repentance (5:19–20); and the nature of true, living faith is expounded (2:18–26). Faith and works are not at odds. Rather, a living faith has/contains works (2:17). Christians who consistently display such a living faith through their humble obedience can be described as perfect (*teleioi*), whole/mature (*holoklēroi*), lacking in nothing (*en mēdeni leipomenoi*) (1:4). James's understanding of faith and works is in accord with the Old Testament Scriptures, the teaching of Jesus in the Gospels, and the other writings of the New Testament.

3

Trials and Temptations

JOB DECLARES THAT AS SURELY as "sparks fly upward," man is born to encounter trouble (Job 5:7). Likewise in his letter, James assumes that Christians will face trials or difficulties in this life and instructs his readers of the proper perspective they should have when those trials come.

The Certainty of Trials

The portions of James's letter that contain words related to trials or temptations (e.g., *peirasmos*, *dokimion*, *dokimos*) come near the beginning of his correspondence (James 1:2–4, 12, 13–15). These instructions serve as a perspectival doorway into the rest of the letter, in which James continues to expound on sundry trials or temptations that Christians will face in this life. We should understand James's initial, more explicit instructions on trials and temptations as theologically programmatic for the rest of the letter.

For example, James condemns the rich man who has defrauded his hired laborers (5:1–6). Addressing the rich oppressor, James writes, "You have laid up treasure in the last days. Behold, the wages of the laborers who mowed your fields, which you kept back by fraud, are crying out against you, and the cries of the harvesters have reached the ears of the Lord of hosts" (5:3–4). A careful reading of James's letter leads to the conclusion that the majority of his addressees would more likely fit in the category of "economically oppressed" rather than "economic oppressor." Thus, even though James does not step aside from his denunciation of the wicked rich to note explicitly that economically oppressed Christians are undergoing a trial, we should understand the apostle's earlier instructions on trials to inform this situation. Indeed, James observes that "the cries of the harvesters have reached the ears of the Lord of hosts" (5:4), reminding his readers that God is aware of the difficulties that poor believers face in this life, he is sovereign over them, and ultimately his righteous and saving purposes are not thwarted even by the wicked actions of powerful and privileged humans. The placement of the following exhortation immediately after James's denunciation of the rich is not accidental: "Be patient, therefore, brothers, until the coming of the Lord. See how the farmer waits for the precious fruit of the earth, being patient about it, until it receives the early and the late rains. You also, be patient. Establish your hearts, for the coming of the Lord is at hand" (5:7–8). This call for believers to be patient (*makrothumeō*) conceptually echoes earlier passages that reference a growing endurance (*hupomonē*) in Christians who face trials (1:3–4).

Let us return, then, to discuss these early paradigmatic texts on trials. After the opening greeting of the letter, James's first words are "Count it all joy, my brothers, when you meet trials of various kinds" (1:2). The apostle communicates several important concepts in this compact statement:

1. By addressing the recipients of the letter as "my brothers" (*adelphoi mou*), James humbly reminds them that he is their spiritual sibling. In using this language, James puts himself under equal obligation to obey the instructions he offers on trials/temptations. This pattern recurs throughout his letter (see 1:19; 2:1, 5, 14; 3:1, 10, 12; 4:11; 5:7, 9, 10, 12, 19).

2. James explicitly qualifies his command with the temporal qualifier *hotan* ("when" or "whenever"). Thus, they are to "count it all joy . . . *when*" they "meet trials [*peirasmois*] of various kinds." It is significant that James does not use a conditional statement ("*if* you meet trials") but an indefinite temporal clause ("*when* you meet trials"). Difficulties and

trials in this life are certain; it is only the timing of the trials and the type and depth of one's suffering that are revealed with the passing of time.

3. James does not just call on his addressees to consider their trials as occassions for "joy" but to consider them as occasions for "*all* joy" (*pasan charan*). This particular use of "all" (*pasan*) marks the "highest degree of something."[1] In other words, Christians should consider a trying and difficult situation as an occasion for the highest degree of joy.

4. What sorts of trials or difficulties is James addressing? He uses a broad qualifier of the trials ("various kinds," *poikilois*). Part of what influenced James's choice of the word *poikilois* ("various kinds") is likely the memorable alliteration of the "p" sound that it created when the text is recited orally in Greek: *peirasmois peripesēte poikilois* ("you meet trials of various kinds"). Furthermore, it is noteworthy what James did not say; he did not say that a Christian should rejoice only when he is persecuted for his faith (cf. Matt 5:11–12; 2 Thess. 1:4–12) or that he should exult only when undergoing physical suffering (2 Cor. 11:23–30). Indeed, the qualifier "various kinds" is broad enough to include any suffering, from comparatively trivial difficulties (e.g., having a minor possession stolen) to life-threatening danger (e.g., severe illness). Christians should view all these trials as an opportunity for supreme joy.

The Sanctifying Effects of Trials

Why are trials, minor or major, an opportunity to count the situation as all joy? James 1:3–4 gives us the answer to this theological conundrum: "For you know that the testing of your faith produces steadfastness. And let steadfastness have its full effect, that you may be perfect and complete, lacking in nothing."

Trials must be viewed as opportunities for supreme joy for the Christian because it is by these difficult experiences that one's faith is tested and the spiritual quality of "steadfastness" (*hypomonē*) is produced.

1 "Πᾶς, πᾶσα, πᾶν," in BDAG 783.

When trials come, the faithful Christian must trust God with matters outside of his or her immediate control—such as one's health, safety, belongings, family, and reputation. In relinquishing the mirage that one can control such aspects of one's own life, the Christian relies more fully on the true sovereign of the universe. Through trials, the Christian develops the fortitude or stick-to-it-ness (*hypomonē*) of spiritual maturity.[2]

Christian steadfastness is not something produced instantaneously. Thus, James commands the letter's recipients, "And let steadfastness have its full effect, that you may be perfect and complete, lacking in nothing" (1:4). A more literal translation reads, "And let endurance have its perfect [*teleion*] work so that you may be perfect [*teleioi*] and complete, lacking in nothing." This more literal translation shows in English the repetition of the word "perfect" (*teleios*) in the Greek construction. And though the Greek third person singular imperative is regularly rendered in English as "let . . . ," the grammatical construction must not be misunderstood as granting permission. It is a command. We might paraphrase: "Make sure, Christians, that you do not shortchange the endurance that God is molding into your life through trials. Continue rejoicing and submitting so that you can see the mature and complete masterpiece that God is working into your life."

As discussed in chapter 2, by using such "perfection" language, James is not teaching perfectionism; rather, he is using hyperbolic language that hints at the glorification of the Christian believer at the end of the age. Even the "perfect," "complete" or "whole" Christian will continue to "stumble in many ways" (James 3:2; cf. 1 John 1:8–10). Nevertheless, over time, there will also be noticeable changes in the lives of Jesus's disciples. These sanctifying changes are what James emphasizes in his letter. While a modern reader might find it odd to use the language of "perfection" (*teleios*) to describe someone who

2 Years ago, I encountered the description of Christian steadfastness as "stick-to-it-ness," but I have not been able to locate the reference.

remains less than literally perfect/sinless, the practice has ample parallels in the works of Philo and the literature of Qumran.[3]

In James 1:12, the apostle unveils an eschatological picture of the eternal fruit of sanctifying trials. He writes, "Blessed is the man who remains steadfast under trial, for when he has stood the test he will receive the crown of life, which God has promised to those who love him." The first word in this verse, "blessed" (*makarios*), has been the subject of significant recent discussion.[4] Despite claims to the contrary, the word frequently conveys the sense of "God's approval rests upon," as the context here clearly favors.[5] The ESV translation, "remains steadfast under," is an apt rendering of the single Greek verb *hypomenei*, which could also be translated as "endures" (NET) or "perseveres" (NASB). What is it, then, that the blessed man endures or perseveres? "Trial" (*peirasmon*). The singular noun is used as the object of the verb in a generic sense. Obviously, a multiplicity of trials over one's life are in view. To paraphrase, James is saying, God's pronouncement of favor (i.e., his pronouncement of "blessing") rests on the Christian who endures in faith and obedience through the sufferings and difficulties of this life.

Trials versus Temptations: Interrelated but Distinct Concepts

If you read the KJV translation of James 1:12, you might be puzzled: "Blessed is the man that endureth temptation: for when he is tried, he shall receive the crown of life, which the Lord hath promised to them that love him." "Temptation?" you might wonder. I thought James was

3 Patrick J. Hartin, *A Spirituality of Perfection: Faith in Action in the Letter of James* (Liturgical, 1999), 26–32.

4 E.g., Jonathan T. Pennington, *The Sermon on the Mount and Human Flourishing: A Theological Commentary* (Baker Academic, 2017), 41–67.

5 Douglas J. Moo notes, "The 'blessing' formula is well known in both the OT (e.g., Ps. 1:1) and the NT (e.g., Matt. 5:3–12). The tendency to translate with the word 'happy' (e.g., TEV, REB) is a misguided effort to avoid unclear 'religious' language and should be resisted. A person who is 'blessed' may not be 'happy' at all. For our emotional state may and will vary with the circumstances of life. But we can be assured that, whatever those circumstances, if we endure them with faith and commitment to God, we will be the recipients of God's favor." Douglas J. Moo, *The Letter of James*, PNTC (Eerdmans, 2000), 69–70.

discussing enduring trials or difficulties. Where did the KJV translators get the word "temptation"? Is there a textual variant here?

No, there is no textual variant. The translational disagreement has to do with the semantic range of the underlying Greek word *peirasmos*. Depending on the context, the word can sometimes carry a more dominant nuance of "difficulty" or "trial." Other times, it carries the idea of "temptation."[6] This is potentially confusing to a modern English reader, as we don't have a word that overlaps with *peirasmos* in semantic range.

English readers without linguistic training may conclude that both senses of trial and temptation are present in every instance of *peirasmos*, but words do not usually function in that way.[7] As Martin Joos notes, "The best meaning is the least meaning."[8] In other words, the most natural, contextually determined meaning that does not introduce new concepts to the discussion is the most likely meaning of a contested word. Most translation committees for modern English Bibles have reached the same decision as the ESV translation committee on James 1:12, rendering *peirasmos* as "trial(s)" (see, e.g., CSB, LSB, NASB, NET, NIV).

It is true, however, that each trial is accompanied by a temptation. Will one trust the sovereign Lord and cry out to him in distress? Or will one give in to despair, faithlessness, or grumbling? Indeed, temptations to sin can be trials of a distinct nature. People facing extreme sexual temptation are undergoing a trial or difficulty in which their bodily desires seem overwhelming, but obedience to God demands that they deny those desires. So while temptations and trials are distinct, we can see how the concepts are interrelated. Dan McCartney argues that the structure of James's letter demands a break between 1:12 and 1:13. Although linked by a "catchword," the instructions are distinct. He

6 "Πειρασμός," in BDAG 793.

7 It does seem, however, that the NLT translators tried to include both senses of *peirasmos* in their translation of James 1:12: "God blesses those who patiently endure testing and temptation. Afterward they will receive the crown of life that God has promised to those who love him."

8 Martin Joos, "Semantic Axiom Number One," *Language* 48, no. 2 (1972): 257, as cited in Moises Silva, *Biblical Words and Their Meaning: An Introduction to Lexical Semantics*, rev. ed. (Zondervan, 1994), 153.

writes, "Note that the testing in 1:12 is a cause for blessedness and is of a different kind than the temptation in 1:13–15, which is a cause of sin."[9]

The Proper Response to Temptations

Trials must be met with faith in the sovereign and good God, resulting in the Christian's growth in endurance, perseverance, or spiritual "stick-to-it-ness." Temptations, on the other hand, require the Christian to resist wicked desires, not shift blame to others, and be aware of the disastrous path to which giving in to temptation leads. James writes,

> Let no one say when he is tempted, "I am being tempted by God," for God cannot be tempted with evil, and he himself tempts no one. But each person is tempted when he is lured and enticed by his own desire. Then desire when it has conceived gives birth to sin, and sin when it is fully grown brings forth death. (1:13–15)

James begins his archetypal passage on temptation by warning against blame shifting. In affirming the sovereignty of God, one must never then make the erroneous theological deduction of attributing wickedness to God. Although God rules over all, he does so in such a way that he can never be blamed for evil. It is impossible to determine if James is aware of people among his addressees who were guilty of blaming God for their temptations or if James just anticipates the problem. Perhaps he explores the theoretical possibility so that he could remind his readers of the character of God. Indeed, reflecting on the character of God provides a theological antigen to temptation. James declares that God is not tempted by evil, nor does he tempt anyone (1:13). Though writing an occasional letter, here James comes close to "theology proper" in his assertion of God's inability to be tempted to sin and his concomitant inability to induce others to sin. A thoughtful Christian may pause to ask how Jesus, the God-man, relates to this verse. One must remember that Jesus had (and has!) two natures, one divine and one human. When the New Testament authors speak of

9 Dan G. McCartney, *James*, BECNT (Baker Academic, 2009),100.

Jesus being tempted (e.g, Luke 4:2), they are speaking of the Savior from the perspective of his human nature. Likewise, when Jesus says, "I thirst" (John 19:28), or "Concerning that day or that hour, no one knows, not even the angels in heaven, nor the Son" (Mark 13:32), he speaks from the perspective of his human nature. Jesus was sinless yet was tempted (in his human nature) in every way like us (Heb. 4:15). Systematic theologians debate the theoretical question as to whether sin was possible for Jesus because of his inherently sinless divine nature. Wayne Grudem observes,

> But the question remains, "How then could Jesus' temptations be real?" The example of the temptation to change the stones into bread is helpful in this regard. Jesus had the ability, by virtue of his divine nature, to perform this miracle, but if he had done it, he would no longer have been obeying in the strength of his human nature alone, he would have failed the test that Adam also failed, and he would not have earned our salvation for us. Therefore, Jesus refused to rely on his divine nature to make obedience easier for him. In like manner, it seems appropriate to conclude that Jesus met every temptation to sin, not by his divine power, but on the strength of his human nature alone (though, of course, it was not "alone" because Jesus, in exercising the kind of faith that humans should exercise, was perfectly depending on God the Father and the Holy Spirit at every moment). The moral strength of his divine nature was there as a sort of "backstop" that would have prevented him from sinning in any case (and therefore we can say that it was not possible for him to sin), but he did not rely on the strength of his divine nature to make it easier for him to face temptations, and his refusal to turn the stones into bread at the beginning of his ministry is a clear indication of this.[10]

"God cannot be tempted with evil, and he himself tempts no one" (James 1:13). Rather, the source of fallen humanity's temptation is an

10 Wayne Grudem, *Systematic Theology: An Introduction to Biblical Doctrine*, 2nd ed. (Zondervan Academic, 2020), 674.

indwelling inclination toward wickedness. This indwelling evil desire can be stoked by worldly allurements (Mark 4:19) or demonic activity (1 Pet. 5:8), but in the end the human agent is to blame for allowing himself to be lured away and enticed. Commentators frequently note the unusual word order of James. The natural chronological progression of temptation is "enticement" followed by "luring away."[11] By reversing the natural chronological progression, James places emphasis on the "luring away." The tragedy of giving in to temptation is that we are dragged away from the realm of true spiritual flourishing—pulled away from the truth, goodness, and love of God's kingdom.

James abruptly shifts to a birth metaphor: "Then desire when it has conceived gives birth to sin, and sin when it is fully grown brings forth death" (1:15). The main point remains the same. Yielding to temptation results in a horrible downward progression—from the desire for evil, to the act of sin, to the sinner's engulfment in the torrent of sin's destruction. Scholars have debated what sort of "death" James speaks of here. Some have proposed that James envisions physical death as temporal punishment for a believer's sin (cf. Acts 5:1–11; 1 Cor 11:29–30).[12] More likely, James again poignantly lays before his readers two ways—one of life and one of death. There is no middle ground, no nuancing, no gray area. The path of yielding to temptation and engaging in sin leads down the road to eternal destruction. By painting in full color the end destination of sin, James warns his readers from taking that path. In actual practice, do believers often yield to sin and then repent? Yes. He tells us as much in other parts of his letter (e.g., "For we all stumble in many ways," James 3:2). Nevertheless, the strength of James's warning against temptation is enhanced by his lack of nuance, footnote, or commentary. Jesus used hyperbole in a similar fashion (Matt. 7:3–5; 18:8–9; 23:24; Luke 14:26).

11 A figure of speech of this sort in which there is an inversion of the natural order of items is called a *hysteron proteron*, which is a transliterated Greek expression meaning "last first."

12 J. A. Motyer claims physical death is part of the referent. J. A. Motyer, *The Message of James*, The Bible Speaks Today (InterVarsity, 1984), 52–54.

Other Biblical Teaching on Trials and Temptations

Within the Old Testament Scriptures, God's sovereignty extends to the smallest details of life (Prov. 16:33) and certainly includes the trials that people face. Moses told the Israelites whom God had rescued out of Egypt that the difficulties they faced in their wilderness wanderings should be viewed under the sovereignty of the covenantal God who was sanctifying them. Moses declared,

> And you shall remember the whole way that the LORD your God has led you these forty years in the wilderness, that he might humble you, testing you to know what was in your heart, whether you would keep his commandments or not. And he humbled you and let you hunger and fed you with manna, which you did not know, nor did your fathers know, that he might make you know that man does not live by bread alone, but man lives by every word that comes from the mouth of the LORD. Your clothing did not wear out on you and your foot did not swell these forty years. Know then in your heart that, as a man disciplines his son, the LORD your God disciplines you. (Deut. 8:2–5)

On an individual basis as well, God's people in the Old Testament era testified to God's sovereignty over their trials and the sanctifying effects of their difficulties. David, the author of Psalm 119, declares to God,

> It is good for me that I was afflicted,
> that I might learn your statutes. (Ps. 119:71)

The story of Joseph (Gen. 37–50) is perhaps one of the most compelling narrative illustrations of trials coming under the sovereignty of God for his people's ultimate good. Although Israel's son Joseph had been mistreated by his brothers, sold into slavery, wrongly accused of sexual assault, and unjustly imprisoned, he did not give in to bitterness or revenge. As ruler of Egypt under Pharaoh (Gen. 41:39–44), and thus capable of inflicting whatever retribution he wished, Joseph instead said to his brothers, "As for you, you meant evil against me, but God meant it for good, to bring it about that many people should be kept alive, as they are today" (Gen. 50:20).

Jesus taught his disciples that both trials and temptations were inevitable in this life. On the night of his betrayal, Jesus told his immediate followers, "I have said these things to you, that in me you may have peace. In the world you will have tribulation. But take heart; I have overcome the world" (John 16:33). The trials and tribulation that Jesus emphasized were the persecutions that his followers would face from hostile outsiders. He warned, "A disciple is not above his teacher, nor a servant above his master. It is enough for the disciple to be like his teacher, and the servant like his master. If they have called the master of the house Beelzebul, how much more will they malign those of his household" (Matt. 10:24–25).

Like tribulation, temptations are certain to come in this fallen age, but that does not mitigate the danger of being a source of them or falling prey to them. Jesus said, "Temptations to sin are sure to come, but woe to the one through whom they come! It would be better for him if a millstone were hung around his neck and he were cast into the sea than that he should cause one of these little ones to sin. Pay attention to yourselves!" (Luke 17:1–3).

Jesus's well-known parable of the sower includes warnings about trials and temptations. In explaining his parable, Jesus said,

> And these are the ones sown on rocky ground: the ones who, when they hear the word, immediately receive it with joy. And they have no root in themselves, but endure for a while; then, when tribulation or persecution arises on account of the word, immediately they fall away. And others are the ones sown among thorns. They are those who hear the word, but the cares of the world and the deceitfulness of riches and the desires for other things enter in and choke the word, and it proves unfruitful. (Mark 4:16–19)

Trials and temptations will come; but for true believers, in the long arc of faithful discipleship, these experiences only serve to sanctify them, make them more fruitful, and bring glory to God. Again, in the parable of the sower, one of the soil types represents faithful believers. About these, Jesus says, "But those that were sown on the good soil are the ones who hear the word and accept it and bear fruit, thirtyfold and sixtyfold and a hundredfold" (Mark 4:20).

It's challenging to think of a more difficult daily trial than the inconveniences and dangers of navigating life without sight. When Jesus was asked by his disciples whether it was a blind man's sin or the sin of his parents that caused his debilitating condition, Jesus replied, "It was not that this man sinned, or his parents, but that the works of God might be displayed in him" (John 9:3). God's sovereignty extended to the trial of this man's blindness, as it extends to the smallest details of life, even a sparrow falling to the ground (Matt. 10:29).

Paul and the rest of the authors of the New Testament agree with James's teaching on trials and temptations. In Paul's warnings to Timothy, we see the certainty of trials, the inevitable presence of temptations, and the need for both endurance and faithfulness:

> But understand this, that in the last days there will come times of difficulty. For people will be lovers of self, lovers of money, proud, arrogant, abusive, disobedient to their parents, ungrateful, unholy, heartless, unappeasable, slanderous, without self-control, brutal, not loving good, treacherous, reckless, swollen with conceit, lovers of pleasure rather than lovers of God, having the appearance of godliness, but denying its power. Avoid such people. For among them are those who creep into households and capture weak women, burdened with sins and led astray by various passions, always learning and never able to arrive at a knowledge of the truth. Just as Jannes and Jambres opposed Moses, so these men also oppose the truth, men corrupted in mind and disqualified regarding the faith. But they will not get very far, for their folly will be plain to all, as was that of those two men. You, however, have followed my teaching, my conduct, my aim in life, my faith, my patience, my love, my steadfastness, my persecutions and sufferings that happened to me at Antioch, at Iconium, and at Lystra—which

> persecutions I endured; yet from them all the Lord rescued me. Indeed, all who desire to live a godly life in Christ Jesus will be persecuted. (2 Tim. 3:1–12)

Space does not permit a full survey of the broader New Testament teaching on trials and temptations. But we should note a statement in Paul's letter to the Galatian Christians that is similar to James's concern for the straying member of the community (James 5:19–20). Paul writes, "Brothers, if anyone is caught in any transgression, you who are spiritual should restore him in a spirit of gentleness. Keep watch on yourself, lest you too be tempted" (Gal. 6:1).

Conclusion

In this broken world, the question is not *whether* Jesus's disciples will face difficulties and temptations but *when* they will face them, to what degree, and how they will respond. James steels his readers with theological truths to prepare them for days of trials and temptations. Most critically, Christians must be aware that God is sovereign over every challenge that comes their way. Christians can rejoice because the diverse trials in their lives are being used by God to strengthen them spiritually and produce the character qualities of endurance or perseverance. When facing temptations, believers need to remember the holy, untemptable character of God (James 1:13) and consider the devastating realities to which giving in to temptation leads (1:15). Such spiritual truths will fortify believers to glorify God through resisting temptation and trusting him in the pressure of trials. James acknowledges that "we all stumble in many ways" (3:2). Nevertheless, our loving heavenly Father is eager to lavish on us the familial reconciliation and forgiveness that restore us to a healthy relationship with him. The placement of language focusing on trials and temptations near the beginning of James's epistle invites us to consider how his instruction on these topics applies to the later issues addressed in his letter. James's teaching on trials and temptations is, in some respects, a perspectival window through which to view the rest of the letter.

4

Poverty and Riches

IT'S COMMON FOR PASTORS to point out (especially during their stewardship sermon series!) that Jesus spoke more about money/wealth than perhaps any other issue.[1] We should not be surprised, then, that Jesus's half-brother James—the early leader of the Jerusalem church and the faithful conveyor of his brother's teaching—also included numerous instructions about money in his short letter.

A Divine Perspective on Poverty and Riches

The first mention of poverty and riches in James's letter (1:9–10) is in the context of the apostle's teaching on trials and the need for divine wisdom to face them with spiritual equanimity (1:2–15). Indeed, both poverty and wealth are spiritual trials, though of different kinds. James calls on his audience to view poverty from a divine perspective in declaring, "Let the lowly brother boast in his exaltation" (1:9). It is clear from the parallel structure of the following verse that the "lowly" (*tapeinos*) brother is one who is in an economically low status. Note also that he is explicitly called a "brother" (*adelphos*). This person is a Christian who has a low socioeconomic status. James instructs this poor brother to boast or exult in his "exaltation" (*hypsos*). James is advising

1 For a scholarly survey of the Bible's teaching on wealth and poverty, see Craig L. Blomberg, *Neither Poverty nor Riches: A Biblical Theology of Possession*, NSBT 7 (InterVarsity Press, 1999).

his poorer readers to take a divine perspective on their temporary lowly status and realize that their heavenly exaltation is imminent (cf. Luke 16:19–31; Eph. 2:6; Col. 2:3; Rev. 6:11).

On the other hand, the rich person should realize how fleeting his earthly status is. The Greek syntax of James 1:10 is staccato in form, as reflected accurately in the ESV translation, "And the rich in his humiliation." Scholars debate whether the ellipsis in Greek (i.e., there is no word "brother" and no verb "boast") implies both the noun and verb from 1:9. If so, the text means that the rich brother should boast in his humiliation. That is, a rich *Christian* is being addressed, and he is likewise being called on to view his exalted earthly status in the same way that God does—temporary and fleeting. The subsequent explanatory clauses in 1:10–11 make clear that the temporary nature of the rich man's status is being emphasized: "Because like a flower of grass he will pass away. For the sun rises with scorching heat and withers the grass." Thus, what is said could apply to Christian or non-Christian wealthy persons. In fact, the language concerning fading away (*marainō*) and humiliation (*tapeinōsis*) perhaps lends itself a bit more readily to being understood as referring to non-Christian wealthy. Regardless of the referent (non-Christian rich or Christian rich), the point stands. Earthly status, privilege, and riches are temporary and fleeting. We should take God's perspective on such matters.

In addressing sinful favoritism (2:1–13), James again calls on his readers to take a divine perspective on poverty and wealth. James assumes that some of his addressees would be tempted to honor a man who comes in with a gold ring and fine clothes.[2] By fawning over him, they would hope to obtain personal favors or future benefits. On the other hand, when a poor man comes in, some would be tempted

2 While modern readers are certainly aware that clothes can convey the status of their wearer, in the ancient world clothes were more directly correlated with an individual's wealth, as each item of clothing was produced by hand, and thus even a simple garment could be a large percentage of an individual's net worth. Note the fascinating paper by David Kotter, "Greater than Gold? How the Value of Clothing Informs the Exegesis of Key New Testament Passages," paper presented at the annual meeting of the Evangelical Theological Society, San Diego, CA, November, 2024.

to neglect him or dishonor him by giving him a less important seat or even having him stand. In doing this, they would be treating the poor man only in view of his potential future economic benefit to them. In exercising such sinful favoritism, James says,

> Have you not then made distinctions among yourselves and become judges with evil thoughts? Listen, my beloved brothers, has not God chosen those who are poor in the world to be rich in faith and heirs of the kingdom, which he has promised to those who love him? But you have dishonored the poor man. Are not the rich the ones who oppress you, and the ones who drag you into court? Are they not the ones who blaspheme the honorable name by which you were called? If you really fulfill the royal law according to the Scripture, "You shall love your neighbor as yourself," you are doing well. But if you show partiality, you are committing sin and are convicted by the law as transgressors. (James 2:4–9)

James calls on his addressees to take a divine perspective on poverty and riches by acknowledging the following: (1) God alone is the one who should judge between persons. (2) God shows special care for the poor, who find themselves in a place of need and call out to him for help. In fact, their poverty turns out to be an unexpected spiritual gift because it makes them trust in God more deeply as their provider and ultimately their Savior. (3) From a practical perspective, showing sycophantic attention to the wicked rich is foolish because the rich will only continue to oppress and mistreat poor Christians. (4) Love for neighbor, as commanded by God (e.g., Lev. 19:18) and ultimately fulfilled in Christ (Matt. 22:36–40; Rom. 13:10; Gal. 5:14), demands that Christians honor and welcome all people, regardless of their socioeconomic status. (5) Partiality shown toward people because of their socioeconomic status is sin.

In James 4:13–17, James condemns the person who says, "Today or tomorrow we will go into such and such a town and spend a year there and trade and make a profit" (4:13). Some readers have wrongly understood this section as generally negative toward business or profit-making. A careful reading of the text shows that it is not entrepreneurial drive or profit that are the problem. The fatal flaw is found here: The entrepreneur's announcement is an example of prideful presumption. James tells us that, contrary to the proud declaration of such plans, "instead you ought to say, 'If the Lord wills, we will live and do this or that'" (4:15). A divine perspective on poverty and riches recognizes that all our economic activities occur under the sovereignty of God and that we are frail, finite creatures who cannot even be sure that we will be alive tomorrow. One's life is mist or smoke (*atmis*) that appears for a little while and then vanishes (4:14).

An Obligation to Assist the Needy

James is insistent that the recipients of his letter, as followers of Jesus Christ, have an obligation to help the needy. He writes, "If anyone thinks he is religious and does not bridle his tongue but deceives his heart, this person's religion is worthless. Religion that is pure and undefiled before God the Father is this: to visit orphans and widows in their affliction, and to keep oneself unstained from the world" (1:26–27).

As we have seen many times, James does not think one's spiritual self-assessment has any value apart from objective external evidence. What sort of religion or spirituality is acceptable and pleasing to God? The first thing James lists is "to visit orphans and widows in their affliction" (1:27). The Greek verb translated "visit" (*episkeptomai*), in this context, clearly does not mean simply to spend time with widows and orphans, though it certainly can't mean less! The verb here has a connotation of visiting "a person with helpful intent."[3] Caring for the widows and orphans takes place in a certain context of need—"in their affliction" (*en tē thlipsei autōn*). In other words, the widows and orphans are facing difficulties and are desperately in need of relief. Modern Christians ensconced in suburban homes are rightly confronted by this text, which challenges us to ask, When was the last time I spent

3 "Ἐπισκέπτομαι," in BDAG 378.

time with orphans or widows? How did I practically provide for their needs? Although one can care for the needs of widows and orphans by clicking a donate button online, James's explicit wording challenges us that our involvement with the poor and needy should more naturally be thought of as involving shared time, experiences, and resources.

Stacy Hare, a missionary in Cameroon, posted this in an online forum on Bible translation:

> If true religion is to visit orphans and widows in their affliction then there is no true religion here. Today I went to a widow's house who just lost her husband last week. She was kept in the dark in the back of the house, dressed in all black, sitting on the floor and not allowed to talk to anyone. She's been like that for days. Other widows are deprived of food, their heads are shaved, and the late husband's family takes all they own: their clothes, fields, dishes, everything. The community simply says they have to suffer like this. When will this place change? When will widows be comforted, provided for, and encouraged? Thankful God is a protector of widows and praying his Spirit would come to this place. Psalm 68:5 "Father of the fatherless and protector of widows is God in his holy habitation."[4]

In James 1:27, "orphans and widows" are illustrative of any person in society who has dire needs and few economically beneficial social connections. Admittedly, there are examples of wealthy widows or orphans who have few, if any, practical needs. (Nevertheless, emotional and social needs are universal!) In thinking through the implications of James's teaching, we can conclude that homeless persons, drug addicts, and the mentally and physically disabled could be added alongside widows and orphans as persons who are greatly in need of being visited by the church—visited both to meet practical needs and to honor the image of God in the person through social interaction and emotional care.

4 Post shared on July 23, 2024, in a private Facebook group of which I am a member. Used with permission.

In James's central passage about faith and works (2:14–26), he begins with an example of a Christian's obligation to care for the practical needs of poorer members of the congregation. James queries,

> What good is it, my brothers, if someone says he has faith but does not have works? Can that faith save him? If a brother or sister is poorly clothed and lacking in daily food, and one of you says to them, "Go in peace, be warmed and filled," without giving them the things needed for the body, what good is that? So also faith by itself, if it does not have works, is dead. (2:14–17)

Thus, we see that when James chooses the foundational example of a living faith that has works, he chooses the issue of (1) a hypothetical impoverished member of the community and (2) a hypothetical member of the community who has the economic resources to help meet the basic needs of an impoverished member. As we have seen repeatedly in James's letter, words alone do not necessarily give a true indication of one's spiritual condition. Words must be accompanied by actions. Indeed, the warm greeting, "Go in peace, be warmed and filled" (2:16) sounds solicitous, if not pious. However, the real test of whether such a greeting is a hollow echo or an expression of genuine warmth is whether the Christian with financial means draws on those resources to provide nourishment and more adequate clothing for the Christian brother or sister in need.

God's Judgment Is Coming on the Wicked Rich

James declares that God will judge the rich who have selfishly hoarded their wealth and economically mistreated others. This theme is most prominent in James 5:

> Come now, you rich, weep and howl for the miseries that are coming upon you. Your riches have rotted and your garments are moth-eaten. Your gold and silver have corroded, and their corrosion will be evidence against you and will eat your flesh like fire. You have laid up

> treasure in the last days. Behold, the wages of the laborers who mowed your fields, which you kept back by fraud, are crying out against you, and the cries of the harvesters have reached the ears of the Lord of hosts. You have lived on the earth in luxury and in self-indulgence. You have fattened your hearts in a day of slaughter. You have condemned and murdered the righteous person. He does not resist you. (5:1–6)

Unlike other hard-hitting portions of James's letter where an indictment of sin is accompanied by an invitation to repentance (e.g., 4:7–10), no possibility of repentance is considered here. Most likely, James is following a prophetic pattern found in the Old Testament prophets in which wicked oppressors outside of the covenant community are condemned (e.g., Amos 1:2–2:3)—both as a matter of consolation to God's people who are suffering and as a warning not to pursue the same rebellious path.[5]

The language in this paragraph is striking. The wicked rich oppressors are taunted that they should weep (*klaiō*) and howl (*ololyzō*) for the miseries that will come upon them. Commentators frequently note that this Greek word for "howl" is found in judgment oracles in the Septuagint.[6] This pattern further supports the conclusion that we have a prophetic statement of judgment against the unrepentant wicked rather than an invitation to turn back to God.

Noteworthy also is the arrestive language in which the riches of the wealthy have "rotted" (*sēpō*, 5:2), their garments are "moth-eaten" (*sētobrōtos*, 5:2), and their gold and silver are "corroded" (*katioō*, 5:3). It is perhaps necessary to observe that these wicked rich people were

5 Calvin writes that James "has a regard to the faithful, that they, hearing of the miserable end of the rich might not envy their fortune, and also that knowing that God would be the avenger of the wrongs they suffered, they might with calm and resigned mind bear them." John Calvin, *Commentaries on the Catholic Epistles*, trans. and ed. John Owen (repr.; Baker, 1999), 342.

6 According to Douglas J. Moo, "*ololyzō* ("wail") is found only in the prophets in the OT and always in the context of judgment (Isa. 10:10; 13:6; 14:31; 15:2–3; 16:7; 23:1, 6, 14; 24:11; 52:5; 65:14; Jer. 2:23; 31:20, 31; Ezek. 2:17; Hos. 7:14; Amos 8:3; Zech. 11:2)." Douglas J. Moo, *The Letter of James*, PNTC (Eerdmans, 2000), 211.

not actually walking around with luxurious clothes filled with holes from moths. And although silver (when not polished) does tarnish, pure gold does not tarnish or corrode. The language is intended to shock the reader by giving a divine perspective on the unrighteously obtained and unrighteously employed wealth of the wicked rich. The money that should have been used to fairly pay employees and assist the needy members of society has instead been, metaphorically speaking, heaped up in a closet. God sees through the dazzling array of clothes and piles of precious metals to the eternal evaluation of how their wealth had been employed, and the wicked rich's stockpile of goods has obtained the grade of F for "fully rotten."

As we continue to consider the striking language of James in this pericope, no indictment is stronger than these words: "You have condemned and murdered the righteous person. He does not resist you" (5:6). Some ancient commentators have detected here a reference to Jesus,[7] who was indeed the only ontologically righteous person to ever live and was murdered by the wealthy and privileged of society. Moreover, Jesus did not resist (1 Pet. 2:23). Yet, James has not given us sufficient contextual markers that he is switching topics to discuss Jesus. Instead, we find here the use of the singular substantive adjective in Greek ("the righteous person," *ton dikaion*) for a generic class of persons. In fact, it is not uncommon for an articular singular substantive to function in this way (e.g., Matt. 12:35; 1 Tim. 3:2). James indicts the wicked rich for exploiting, condemning (through unjust use of power and connections), and murdering (through deprivation of the most basic provisions) the *comparatively* (not ontologically) righteous poor laborer who works for him. We find similar hyperbolic and prophetic denunciation of the rich in Second Temple Jewish literature. For example, in Sirach 34:24–27 we read,

> Like one who slaughters a son in the presence of his father
> is the man who offers a sacrifice from the property of the poor.

7 Oecumenius, Bede, and Cassiodorus, as cited by Moo, *The Letter of James*, 218n8.

> The bread of the needy is the life of the poor;
> whoever deprives them of it is a man of blood.
> To take away a neighbor's living is to murder him;
> to deprive an employee of his wages is to shed blood.[8]

Following the condemnation of the wicked rich—a message "overheard" by the faithful to whom James writes—we find a passage directed to these believers who are suffering:

> Be patient, therefore, brothers, until the coming of the Lord. See how the farmer waits for the precious fruit of the earth, being patient about it, until it receives the early and the late rains. You also, be patient. Establish your hearts, for the coming of the Lord is at hand. Do not grumble against one another, brothers, so that you may not be judged; behold, the Judge is standing at the door. As an example of suffering and patience, brothers, take the prophets who spoke in the name of the Lord. Behold, we consider those blessed who remained steadfast. You have heard of the steadfastness of Job, and you have seen the purpose of the Lord, how the Lord is compassionate and merciful. (James 5:7–11)

James's call to patience echoes the beginning of his letter in which believers are told to consider it all joy whenever they face many trials because the testing of their faith develops steadfastness (1:2–3). Being oppressed by wicked and powerful people is a trial that has been faced by many of God's covenant people over the past millennia. James promises no quick and easy fix of this plight for his spiritual siblings. (Note again how James addresses the recipients of the letter as "brothers," *adelphoi*. James and his recipients are members of the same spiritual family, living in an unjust world that is groaning for the Creator to set all things right [Rom. 8:22].) Followers of Jesus, James tells us, must exercise patience "until the coming of the Lord." As I noted in chapter 1,

8 *ESV Apocrypha Text Edition* (Cambridge University Press, 2021), 96.

James is likely referring to the parousia—the second coming of Christ and all it entails. Ever the colorful preacher, James illustrates his exhortation to patience with agricultural and climatological comparisons (James 5:7). Then, he repeats his initial command with slight variations: "Establish your hearts, for the coming of the Lord is at hand" (5:8). Indeed, how can one keep one's head up and faith intact when being mistreated and dehumanized by powerful people and unjust circumstances for which there is no recourse in this life? It is by remembering that, in the final analysis, "the coming of the Lord is at hand" (5:8). Just as David was able to forsake resentment, leave retribution to the Lord, and thus treat Saul with undeserved kindness (e.g., 1 Sam. 24:4–11), so also Christians can entrust their vindication to God, knowing that at Christ's return all will be made right. Our hearts will not fail us as we rest on these sure promises.

Other Biblical Teaching on Poverty and Riches

In addressing the issues of wealth and poverty, God's prior revelation is cut from the same theological cloth as the epistle of James. Although wealth can be a sign of God's temporal blessing in this life (Gen. 24:35; 1 Kings 3:13; 1 Chron. 29:12), riches are consistently described as uncertain, fleeting, and deceptive (Ps. 39:6; Prov. 11:38; 23:4–5; 27:24; Eccl. 5:10; Jer. 17:11). The author of Proverbs warns,

> Do not toil to acquire wealth;
>   be discerning enough to desist.
> When your eyes light on it, it is gone,
>   for suddenly it sprouts wings,
>   flying like an eagle toward heaven. (Prov. 23:4–5)

The life of Gehazi, the servant of Elisha, provides a poignant case study of a person whose views on wealth did not align with the divine perspective. The prophet Elisha refused to accept compensation from the Syrian general Naaman for his supernatural healing from leprosy. Later, Gehazi secretly ran after Naaman and deceitfully acquired for himself two talents of silver and two changes of clothing. After hiding his loot, Gehazi approached Elisha, who asked,

> "Where have you been, Gehazi?" And he said, "Your servant went nowhere." But he said to him, "Did not my heart go when the man turned from his chariot to meet you? Was it a time to accept money and garments, olive orchards and vineyards, sheep and oxen, male servants and female servants? Therefore the leprosy of Naaman shall cling to you and to your descendants forever." So he went out from his presence a leper, like snow. (2 Kings 5:25–27)

Gehazi failed to honor the word of the Lord through the prophet Elisha, who had declared that no gift would be accepted from Naaman for the healing that *the Lord* had done (2 Kings 5:16). Proverbs 19:1 speaks to the temptation and sin that beset Gehazi:

> Better is a poor person who walks in his integrity
> than one who is crooked in speech and is a fool.

Within the Old Testament, there is a consistent expectation that wealthier members of God's covenant community are obligated to care for those in need. Divine stipulations required farmers to leave the edges of their fields ungleaned for the poor so that they would be able to gather food for themselves (Lev. 19:9–10; 23:22; Deut. 24:19–21). In like manner, God explicitly permits persons to pick grains or fruits for immediate consumption as they walk through a neighbor's field, although gathering food in baskets or containers from a neighbor's field is forbidden (Deut. 23:24–25). In deciding court cases, judges are barred from considering the economic or social status of the person being judged (Ex. 23:2–3). They are not to "lift the face of the poor"—the Hebrew idiom translated as "be partial to the poor" (Lev. 19:15). In other words, justice is to be blind or impartial in its application.

Perhaps even more radical than the laws discussed above were the provisions for the year of jubilee, in which debts were canceled and ancestral lands were returned (Lev. 25:8–17). The Old Testament emphasizes individual responsibility and private property rights, but it is also sometimes surprisingly radical in its call to care for the poor and prevent the concentration of wealth or property ownership in too few hands (e.g., through returning ancestral lands every forty-nine years). There is scant evidence from Israel's history that the ancient Israelites obeyed these radical economic requirements; rather they are condemned for neglecting them. The prophet Isaiah declares,

> Woe to those who join house to house,
>   who add field to field,
> until there is no more room,
>   and you are made to dwell alone
>   in the midst of the land. (Isa. 5:8)

Beyond the specific legal stipulations and prophetic censures, generosity was enjoined as a way of life pleasing to God. Proverbs 19:17 declares,

> Whoever is generous to the poor lends to the LORD,
>   and he will repay him for his deed.

Just as James declares the certainty of God's coming judgment for the wicked rich, so does the Old Testament. The language of the minor prophets is especially striking. Amos declares God's oracle of judgment against the wicked rich:

> Therefore because you trample on the poor
>   and you exact taxes of grain from him,
> you have built houses of hewn stone,
>   but you shall not dwell in them;
> you have planted pleasant vineyards,
>   but you shall not drink their wine.
> For I know how many are your transgressions
>   and how great are your sins—

you who afflict the righteous, who take a bribe,
and turn aside the needy in the gate. (Amos 5:11–12)

Similarly, about the morally corrupt wealthy in his day, the prophet Micah says,

Woe to those who devise wickedness
and work evil on their beds!
When the morning dawns, they perform it,
because it is in the power of their hand.
They covet fields and seize them,
and houses, and take them away;
they oppress a man and his house,
a man and his inheritance.
Therefore thus says the LORD:
behold, against this family I am devising disaster,
from which you cannot remove your necks,
and you shall not walk haughtily,
for it will be a time of disaster.
In that day they shall take up a taunt song against you
and moan bitterly,
and say, "We are utterly ruined;
he changes the portion of my people;
how he removes it from me!
To an apostate he allots our fields." (Mic. 2:1–4)

As noted at the beginning of this chapter, Jesus frequently addressed the topic of wealth and financial stewardship in his ministry. The limitations of this study do not allow us to explore in detail Jesus's teaching on wealth and poverty, but we can see that the same Jacobean themes appear in his teaching. (Obviously, the original setting of Jesus's teaching chronologically precedes James.) God cares for the poor and outcast (Luke 4:18–19); indeed, a divine benediction is pronounced on the economically poor who thus more easily perceive their spiritual poverty and look to God in trust (Luke 6:20). Wealthy persons who are not "rich toward God" (Luke 12:21) can expect only condemnation and punishment (Luke 12:16–20). The life of the rich man is as tenuous as a thin thread that could break at any time (Luke 12:20). Furthermore, Jesus warned that the riches that people wrongly rely on encrust their hearts and make it impossible for them to respond to the gospel, apart from the supernatural intervention of God (Matt. 19:24–25).

When not unrighteously obtained, money can be a great blessing from God, but the multiplicity of warnings in Scripture should give the wealthy person great pause and renewed commitment to use his resources for eternal purposes. Jesus warned,

> Do not lay up for yourselves treasures on earth, where moth and rust destroy and where thieves break in and steal, but lay up for yourselves treasures in heaven, where neither moth nor rust destroys and where thieves do not break in and steal. For where your treasure is, there your heart will be also. (Matt. 6:19–21)

Jesus's teaching on wealth accords with the rest of the New Testament, including the instructions of the apostle Paul, who provided this nuanced teaching on wealth to his protégé Timothy:

> As for the rich in this present age, charge them not to be haughty, nor to set their hopes on the uncertainty of riches, but on God, who richly provides us with everything to enjoy. They are to do good, to be rich in good works, to be generous and ready to share, thus storing up treasure for themselves as a good foundation for the future, so that they may take hold of that which is truly life. (1 Tim. 6:17–19)

Conclusion

Throughout human history, people have frequently found themselves in a state of poverty. Few have lived in wealth. A prosperous, sizeable middle class is a relatively recent phenomenon. Most humans have lived in one of two worlds—deprivation (the majority of people) or abundance (a few). James speaks with poignancy and divine wisdom to the timeless realities of poverty and wealth. God cares for the poor man who, if he belongs to God's people, will soon (in the coming age) see a reversal of his fortunes (James 1:9–11). The wicked rich will soon be undone (5:1–6). In light of these realities, God's people should actively love their poor neighbors in tangible ways (2:14–26). James's teaching on wealth and poverty accords with the Old Testament, the teaching of Jesus, and the rest of the New Testament writings.

5

Speech and Anger

THE RENOWNED JACOBEAN SCHOLAR Peter Davids customarily told his students that they could not really understand the epistle of James until they read the Jewish apocryphal work Sirach/Ecclesiasticus.[1] The point Davids was trying to make (provocatively!), I think, was that much of James's epistle reads like proverbial Jewish literature, and a familiarity with that genre is helpful for proper interpretation.

Two of the main themes or motifs that we find in Jewish proverbial literature are (1) the dangers of wicked speech (e.g., Prov. 4:24; 6:17 10:18; 11:9; 12:18) and (2) the hazards of unrighteous anger and strife (e.g., Prov. 6:19; 15:1, 18; 16:32; 19:11; 20:3). Thus, it is not surprising that we find these two themes prominently featured in the epistle of James. Although I address these two topics sequentially and topically in this chapter, it is worth reflecting on the wisdom of God in providentially leading James to scatter reflections on these topics throughout his letter. It is often by repeated exposure to a topic, interspersed by the discussion of other issues, that the matter under consideration is driven down deep into a reader's consciousness.

The Danger of Sinful Speech

James repeatedly circles back in his letter to warn against sinful speech (James 1:19, 26; 3:1–12; 4:11–12; 5:12). The longest and most centrally

1 Peter Davids, email message to the author, July 23, 2024.

located of these passages is 3:1–12. For a topical treatment of James's teaching on speech ethics, perhaps it is wisest to start our study here:

> Not many of you should become teachers, my brothers, for you know that we who teach will be judged with greater strictness. For we all stumble in many ways. And if anyone does not stumble in what he says, he is a perfect man, able also to bridle his whole body. If we put bits into the mouths of horses so that they obey us, we guide their whole bodies as well. Look at the ships also: though they are so large and are driven by strong winds, they are guided by a very small rudder wherever the will of the pilot directs. So also the tongue is a small member, yet it boasts of great things.
>
> How great a forest is set ablaze by such a small fire! And the tongue is a fire, a world of unrighteousness. The tongue is set among our members, staining the whole body, setting on fire the entire course of life, and set on fire by hell. For every kind of beast and bird, of reptile and sea creature, can be tamed and has been tamed by mankind, but no human being can tame the tongue. It is a restless evil, full of deadly poison. With it we bless our Lord and Father, and with it we curse people who are made in the likeness of God. From the same mouth come blessing and cursing. My brothers, these things ought not to be so. Does a spring pour forth from the same opening both fresh and salt water? Can a fig tree, my brothers, bear olives, or a grapevine produce figs? Neither can a salt pond yield fresh water. (3:1–12)

Although this passage appears to be addressed to the congregation more generally, it begins with a reference specifically to teachers.[2] James's instructions on speech are especially applicable to teachers in the church because, by nature of their role, teachers speak more words than the average congregant. And because teachers speak more and do so in an authoritative and influential way, if their words are sinful or

2 Dave DeKlavon, a former colleague, once wryly observed, "Of course, not many people should become teachers (James 3:1) because then there would be too many teachers, and we might lose our jobs!"

erroneous, there is potentially much harm done to their pupils. James tells us that God holds teachers accountable for words that harm others or lead them astray.

In the image-saturated passage of 3:1–12, the apostle holds out the example of the "perfect" (*teleios*) man who does not stumble in his speech and, thus, is able to keep all other parts of his body in check (3:2). Along with James's other passages that use "perfect" terminology (1:4, 25), we should likely understand that in 3:2 James is intending to set before his readers an achievable status. He describes a mature Christian whose speech is consistently (not perfectly!) true, kind, and helpful. James does not describe someone who literally never sins in speech because no such person—except for the Lord Jesus—has ever existed or will exist in this fallen age. In support of this interpretation, we find that James's praise of the "perfect" man is accompanied by a realistic qualification that "we all stumble in many ways" (3:2). (See the discussion of James's "perfect" language in chapter 1.)

As a gifted communicator, James employs striking images that help make his teaching memorable and affective (i.e., producing an emotional response). The human tongue is tiny—like a bit in the mouth of a horse or a small rudder steering a huge ship—but what gigantic effects it can have on the speaker and those around him! Just as a spark can set a whole forest ablaze, a wicked tongue can leave behind widespread destruction. Indeed, if we are willing to admit how the speech of fallen humans usually functions, the words of James ring poignantly true: "No human being can tame the tongue. It is a restless evil, full of deadly poison" (3:8).

Repeatedly calling out hypocrisy in his letter, James points out the spiritual inconsistency found in many believers' speech patterns. The apostle writes, "With [the tongue] we bless our Lord and Father, and with it we curse people who are made in the likeness of God. From the same mouth come blessing and cursing. My brothers, these things ought not to be so" (3:9–10). James ends this passage with a panoply of natural images (i.e., a spring of water, a salt pond, fresh water, salt water, a fig tree, olives, a grapevine, figs) to emphasize the point that spiritual constancy demands that we speak truthfully and respectfully about both God and people made in his image. Just as a fig tree bears figs, a grapevine bears grapes, and a natural spring pours forth fresh water, followers of Jesus should only speak words that are truthful, kind, and loving.

Having considered the longest passage on speech ethics in the letter (3:1–12), we will now briefly survey James's other teachings on communication scattered throughout the epistle. In 1:19 James declares that disciples of Jesus should be eagerly attentive in their listening to others and not in a rush to speak. In 1:26 the apostle condemns the incongruity of thinking oneself religious while not also being restrained and godly in one's speech. (This brief comment on spiritual consistency early in James's letter anticipates his fuller treatment in 3:1–12.) In 4:11 he warns against slandering or engaging in other judgmental or wicked speech toward another member of the Christian community. Disciples of Jesus are to be doers of the law, not judges who beat down others with words of condemnation. God alone is judge (4:12). Finally, in 5:12, mirroring almost the exact words of Jesus in Matthew 5:34–37, James forbids the taking of any oaths.

Looking more broadly at the topic of oaths/swearing in the New Testament, it seems that the apostles and even Jesus took oaths or submitted to being put under oaths (Matt. 26:63–64; 2 Cor. 11:31; Gal. 1:20; Phil. 1:8). In Jesus's discussion of oaths in the Gospels (Matt. 5:33–37; 23:16–22), the focus of his concern is not on forbidding oaths but casuistry—that is, the employment of an oath as a means for dissembling. To the scribes and Pharisees, Jesus said, "Woe to you, blind guides, who say, 'If anyone swears by the temple, it is nothing, but if anyone swears by the gold of the temple, he is bound by his oath.' You blind fools! For which is greater, the gold or the temple that has made the gold sacred?" (Matt. 23:16–17). Oaths were being employed to misrepresent reality to others. At the same time, the use of any oath is the implicit admission that human speech is often deceptive. Humans would never need to swear oaths if their speech were consistently truthful and forthright.

How might a modern follower of Jesus who is seeking to obey James's and Jesus's teachings on oaths respond to the request that he swear an oath before testifying in a courtroom? If a Christian wanted to be dramatic in the courtroom, he might declare, "I do not object to swearing to tell the truth, but as a Christian, my words are always to be truthful, so publicly swearing to tell the truth makes no difference in how I speak."[3]

Some Christian traditions, such as the Mennonites, accept literally James's and Jesus's prohibitions of oaths. To swear an oath, even for a formal civic responsibility, is considered direct disobedience of Scripture and thus a sin. As an accommodation to the consciences of people with such religious convictions, Mennonites and other like-minded Christians are often allowed to affirm their convictions without any formal swearing or oath taking. If you are not convinced of my discussion of oaths, then you should follow the dictates of your conscience. As the Reformer Martin Luther famously declared at the Diet (Assembly) of Worms (1521), "To go against conscience is neither right nor safe."[4]

The Danger of Anger

The book of Proverbs warns against unrighteous anger and strife. Consider the following sample proverbs addressing these matters:

> A soft answer turns away wrath,
> but harsh words stir up anger. (Prov. 15:1)
>
> A hot-tempered man stirs up strife,
> but he who is slow to anger quiets contention. (Prov. 15:18)
>
> Whoever is slow to anger is better than the mighty,
> and he who rules his spirit than he who takes a city. (Prov. 16:32)

3 I am influenced by my hermeneutical mentor, Robert Stein, in my explanation here.
4 Roland H. Bainton, *Here I Stand: A Life of Martin Luther* (Abingdon, 1950), 144.

> Good sense makes one slow to anger,
> and it is his glory to overlook an offense. (Prov. 19:11)
>
> It is better to live in a desert land
> than with a quarrelsome and fretful woman. (Prov. 21:19)

James expresses the same perspective on sinful anger and human strife, though he does not deal with the topic as extensively as he covers speech ethics.

As is typical for wisdom literature, neither Proverbs nor the letter of James deals with all the nuances of anger. In other words, these ancient works do not lay out all the possible reasons for anger and how those categories should be thought of differently. We must admit that most human anger is tied to selfishness and sin. Both Proverbs and James focus on such unrighteous anger. However, it is also important to note that God is frequently described as wrathful or angry in Scripture (e.g., Ex. 22:24; Num. 11:1; Deut. 9:7–8). Obviously, divine anger is without sin (Deut. 32:4; Job 34:10; Ps. 92:15; James 1:13). In fact, divine wrath can be thought of as God's settled opposition to sin.[5] Sometimes commentators also point out that humans can mirror God in his righteous anger toward sin and injustice. The newly anointed King Saul apparently displayed a moment of truly righteous anger when he heard of the Ammonite's besieging of Jabesh-gilead:

> Now, behold, Saul was coming from the field behind the oxen. And Saul said, "What is wrong with the people, that they are weeping?" So they told him the news of the men of Jabesh. And the Spirit of God rushed upon Saul when he heard these words,

5 Wayne Grudem writes, "It may surprise us to find out how frequently the Bible talks about the wrath of God. Yet if God loves all that is right and good, and all that conforms to his moral character, then it should not be surprising that he would hate everything that is opposed to his moral character. God's wrath directed against sin is therefore closely related to God's holiness and justice. God's wrath may be defined as follows: *God's wrath means that he intensely hates sin*." Wayne Grudem, *Systematic Theology: An Introduction to Biblical Doctrine*, 2nd ed. (Zondervan Academic, 2020), 245.

> and his anger was greatly kindled. He took a yoke of oxen and cut them in pieces and sent them throughout all the territory of Israel by the hand of the messengers, saying, "Whoever does not come out after Saul and Samuel, so shall it be done to his oxen!" Then the dread of the LORD fell upon the people, and they came out as one man. (1 Sam. 11:5–7)

The apostle Paul also seems to envision the possibility of righteous human anger when he says, "Be angry and do not sin; do not let the sun go down on your anger" (Eph. 4:26). Yet, even when human anger is rightly directed at injustice or sin, rarely does it fail to veer into sin itself. It is this reality of tainted human anger that James is keen to address. When I speak of "anger" below (mirroring James's wording), I am referring to human anger tainted by sin, not to holy wrath or righteous indignation.

James's first direct reference to human anger or community strife is in James 1:19–22, where he writes,

> Know this, my beloved brothers: let every person be quick to hear, slow to speak, slow to anger; for the anger of man does not produce the righteousness of God. Therefore put away all filthiness and rampant wickedness and receive with meekness the implanted word, which is able to save your souls.
>
> But be doers of the word, and not hearers only, deceiving yourselves.

I've included additional context to demonstrate that James classifies sinful human anger with the categories of "filthiness" and "rampant wickedness," from which his addressees are called to repent. Giving in to sinful human anger is a manifestation of not being a "doer of the word"; it is an act of disobedience to God's commands to not be angry with others and to live at peace (see Lev. 19:9–18; Rom. 12:18; James 3:17–18). To express sinful human anger without repentance is to be a self-deceived person, to hear the word and not do it.

James uses an imperative in 1:19: "Be . . . slow to anger." In other words, he exhorts these Christians to constantly pour water on the fires of anger that well up in their fleshly response to annoyances or challenges. In contrast to the spirit of the modern age, James does not call on Christians to be "authentic" to their feelings but rather to recognize sinful anger for what it is, suppress it, repent of it, and strive for peace.

James could have appealed to the nature of God (e.g., Ex. 34:6; Num. 14:18; Neh. 9:17) or to prior Old Testament revelation (e.g., Prov. 14:29; 15:8; Eccl. 7:9) as the grounds for his command to be slow to anger. Instead, he offers a theological argument grounded in logic (and, one might argue, experiential observation as well): "For the anger of man does not produce the righteousness of God" (James 1:20). We could paraphrase these words accordingly: "Human anger does not produce the righteous life that God wants his people to live." James is consistently concerned with the practical manifestation of one's spirituality, and this text is no exception. Human anger tainted by sin is itself a transgression. Moreover, it is a sin that spills over into other aspects of a person's life, preventing the harvest of righteousness that God desires to see in the lives of his peacemaking people (3:18).

The next two passages we will look at address more directly strife or quarrels within the community. In 3:14–18 James writes,

> But if you have bitter jealousy and selfish ambition in your hearts, do not boast and be false to the truth. This is not the wisdom that comes down from above, but is earthly, unspiritual, demonic. For where jealousy and selfish ambition exist, there will be disorder and every vile practice. But the wisdom from above is first pure, then peaceable, gentle, open to reason, full of mercy and good fruits, impartial and sincere. And a harvest of righteousness is sown in peace by those who make peace.

In this text, James contrasts true wisdom, shown by a life of faith, obedience, and human tranquility, with a worldly "wisdom" characterized by human strife and relational disorder. The reader should remember that in the ancient Semitic context of James's writing, wisdom was not an academic discipline that considered esoteric philosophical questions. Rather, wisdom was about discovering the right ultimate orientation of one's life, resulting in a life well lived.

When humans discover relational disorder and vile practices within their communities, where should they look to lay the blame? James says to look within yourselves—in your own hearts—for out of hearts filled with jealousy and selfish ambition flow community strife and sinful behavior. On the other hand, for persons whose values are determined by their loyalty to the Lord Jesus, we should expect to find relational harmony. The characteristics with which James labels such persons are the opposite of strife: "peaceable, gentle, open to reason, full of mercy and good fruits, impartial and sincere" (3:17).

Following 3:14–18, James continues addressing human strife: "What causes quarrels and what causes fights among you? Is it not this, that your passions are at war within you? You desire and do not have, so you murder. You covet and cannot obtain, so you fight and quarrel. You do not have, because you do not ask" (4:1–2). As with the text above, the emphasis is on the origin of strife within the community. In situations where individuals or groups are fighting, it is so easy to point fingers at the other side. Instead, James says believers must look within themselves for the fundamental cause of discord in the community. Strife is a manifestation of their selfish desires. In describing pugnacious Christians as committing "murder," James surely intends the language metaphorically. The believers to whom he writes are not literally killing each other. But their selfish squabbling is, in essence, embryonic murder through the hatred and disregard they show for others. The shocking language is reminiscent of Jesus's statements in the Sermon on the Mount (e.g., Matt. 5:27–28: "You have heard that it was said, 'You shall not commit adultery.' But I say to you that everyone who looks at a woman with lustful intent has already committed adultery with her in his heart").

What is James's solution to Christians driven by selfishness and living in strife? Most fundamentally, he calls them to repentance:

> Submit yourselves therefore to God. Resist the devil, and he will flee from you. Draw near to God, and he will draw near to you. Cleanse your hands, you sinners, and purify your hearts, you double-minded. Be wretched and mourn and weep. Let your laughter be turned to mourning and your joy to gloom. Humble yourselves before the Lord, and he will exalt you. (4:7–10)

In this extended call to repentance, James demands both a recognition of one's personal culpability for selfishness and strife as well as the recognition that we have a powerful spiritual enemy ("the devil," 4:7) who deceives and influences humans toward wickedness.

In the style of pronouncements in wisdom literature, James does not nuance his discussion. Anger and strife are rooted in sinful desires, often influenced by the devil, and must be repented of. To turn away from anger and community discord is to turn back toward God who exalts the humble transgressor who comes to him in repentance.

Other Biblical Teaching on Speech and Anger

As noted above, the book of Proverbs is filled with admonitions against wicked speech and sinful human anger (e.g., Prov 6:16–19; 10:18; 11:9; 12:18; 14:17; 15:1, 18, 16:28, 32; 18:21; 19:19; 20:19; 22:24–25; 26:20). Outside of Proverbs, divine disapproval of wicked speech and sinful anger is usually not stated as an aphorism, yet God's approach to these issues is consistent in the Old Testament. Leviticus 19 is an interesting place to explore these topics, as so much material in the letter of James overlaps with the content of Leviticus 19.[6] Several places in the chapter condemn wicked speech:

- "You shall not deal falsely; you shall not lie to one another" (Lev. 19:11).

6 See Luke Timothy Johnson, "The Use of Leviticus 19 in the Letter of James," in *Brother of Jesus, Friend of God: Studies in the Letter of James* (Eerdmans, 2004), 122–35.

- "You shall not swear by my name falsely, and so profane the name of your God: I am the LORD" (Lev. 19:12).
- "You shall not curse the deaf or put a stumbling block before the blind, but you shall fear your God: I am the LORD" (Lev. 19:14).
- "You shall not go around as a slanderer among your people, and you shall not stand up against the life of your neighbor: I am the LORD" (Lev. 19:16).

Likewise, several texts in Leviticus 19 condemn sinful anger or strife:

- "You shall not hate your brother in your heart, but you shall reason frankly with your neighbor, lest you incur sin because of him" (Lev. 19:17).
- "You shall not take vengeance or bear a grudge against the sons of your own people, but you shall love your neighbor as yourself: I am the LORD" (Lev. 19:18).

There are many other Old Testament texts that condemn sinful speech, human anger, and community strife (e.g., Gen. 49:6–7; Pss. 34:13; 52:2–4; 101:5; 120:2–3; Eccl. 7:9), but the brief list of texts from Leviticus 19 is sufficient to show that the letter of James is cut from the same cloth as God's previous revelation.

James's letter also accords with Jesus's teaching on speech, anger, and strife. Jesus warned, "I tell you, on the day of judgment people will give account for every careless word they speak, for by your words you will be justified, and by your words you will be condemned" (Matt. 12:36–37). Likewise, Jesus strongly condemned anger and strife:

> You have heard that it was said to those of old, "You shall not murder; and whoever murders will be liable to judgment." But I say to you that everyone who is angry with his brother will be liable to judgment; whoever insults his brother will be liable to the council; and whoever says, "You fool!" will be liable to the hell of fire. So if

> you are offering your gift at the altar and there remember that your brother has something against you, leave your gift there before the altar and go. First be reconciled to your brother, and then come and offer your gift. Come to terms quickly with your accuser while you are going with him to court, lest your accuser hand you over to the judge, and the judge to the guard, and you be put in prison. Truly, I say to you, you will never get out until you have paid the last penny. (Matt. 5:21–26)

Jesus's teaching on speech, anger, and strife accords with the rest of the apostolic witness in the New Testament. For example, Paul writes,

> Therefore, having put away falsehood, let each one of you speak the truth with his neighbor, for we are members one of another. Be angry and do not sin; do not let the sun go down on your anger, and give no opportunity to the devil. Let the thief no longer steal, but rather let him labor, doing honest work with his own hands, so that he may have something to share with anyone in need. Let no corrupting talk come out of your mouths, but only such as is good for building up, as fits the occasion, that it may give grace to those who hear. And do not grieve the Holy Spirit of God, by whom you were sealed for the day of redemption. Let all bitterness and wrath and anger and clamor and slander be put away from you, along with all malice. Be kind to one another, tenderhearted, forgiving one another, as God in Christ forgave you. (Eph. 4:25–32)

The New Testament is filled with practical exhortation on speech, anger, and strife (e.g., Rom. 12:18; 1 Cor. 1:10; Gal. 5:19–20; Phil. 2:14; Col. 3:8; 1 Tim. 5:13; 2 Tim. 2:16, 23–24; Titus 1:7; 3:2; 1 Pet. 3:10).

Conclusion

All humans (including Christians) sin against one another through wicked speech, sinful anger, and relational strife. James addresses these common sins and calls for his Christian brothers and sisters to repent of such evil, resist the devil, and turn back to God in humility and trusting obedience. James's assessments and prescriptions for sins of speech, anger, and strife are in accord with the Old Testament, the teachings of Jesus, and the apostolic writings in the New Testament.

6
Prayer

AS JAMES ADDRESSES SO MANY practical aspects of the Christian life in his letter, we should not be surprised that he includes several sections that focus on prayer (James 1:5–8; 4:2–3; 5:13–18). Modern readers of James's epistle are challenged not only to conform their prayers to the apostle's explicit instructions about intercession but also to allow all the letter's teaching to shape the content and tenor of their petitions.

Prayer for Wisdom

The first passage in James that explicitly addresses prayer instructs the letter's recipients to ask for wisdom if they lack it:

> If any of you lacks wisdom, let him ask God, who gives generously to all without reproach, and it will be given him. But let him ask in faith, with no doubting, for the one who doubts is like a wave of the sea that is driven and tossed by the wind. For that person must not suppose that he will receive anything from the Lord; he is a double-minded man, unstable in all his ways. (1:5–8)

We approach the paragraph asking what it tells us about prayer (see chap. 2 for a discussion of the passage regarding the topic of deficient faith). We discover: (1) Prayer should be offered for wisdom. Biblically, wisdom encompasses both practical knowledge and a flourishing life lived in reverence for God. Immediately after the quoted passage above, James enjoins a divine perspective on wealth and poverty. Indeed, to truly view wealth from a divine perspective, we need supernatural wisdom. Thus, James tells us, it is good and right to pray for such wisdom. (2) Petitions should be offered "in faith" (James 1:6). In other words, when we pray to God, we must believe that he is good, powerful, and kindly disposed toward the petitions of his people. Yes, we submit all our requests to his will (1 John 5:14), but when God's word has already made clear that he wants to give his people wisdom (James 1:5), we can ask for wisdom with an absolute certainty of God's response. (3) Praying with doubt in God's goodness, power, or kind inclination is displeasing to God, and the doubting petitioner should not expect to receive anything from the Lord. Considering the content of supplications more broadly, the lack of a positive response from God does not necessarily indicate a deficiency in the petitioner. A fully developed theology of prayer must consider more than this brief text in James.

Prayer for Practical Needs

While wisdom is certainly a spiritual necessity, the next prayer text we will consider envisions more tangible needs for which the Christian prays (see the discussion of this passage in chap. 5 for James's instructions on anger and strife).

> What causes quarrels and what causes fights among you? Is it not this, that your passions are at war within you? You desire and do not have, so you murder. You covet and cannot obtain, so you fight and quarrel. You do not have, because you do not ask. You ask and do not receive, because you ask wrongly, to spend it on your passions. (4:1–3)

James addresses directly the greed and coveting that are often at the root of community strife. When a Christian realizes a need, whether from looking within or seeing God's provision in the lives of others, the first thing that a believer should do is to ask God. Indeed, James says, "You do not have, because you do not ask" (4:2). This memorable maxim exposes the practical atheism of many Christians' lives. Rather than turning to their heavenly Father in their needs and desires, they take matters into their own hands, seething in jealousy or hurting others in an attempt to get what they want.

In the few instances where these greedy, contentious people petition God, they do so in a deeply flawed way. James writes, "You ask and do not receive, because you ask wrongly, to spend it on your passions" (James 4:3). This verse is reminiscent of the episode in the Gospels where Jesus was asked to arbitrate an inheritance dispute. He replied, "Man, who made me a judge or arbitrator over you?" (Luke 12:14). Fitting to such a request, Jesus followed up, "Take care, and be on your guard against all covetousness, for one's life does not consist in the abundance of his possessions" (Luke 12:15). Not only the content of our requests but also the disposition of our hearts is of concern to our heavenly Father. God is not interested in forming us into selfish, greedy hypocrites. Not answering our prayers could be one of the best things that he could do for our sanctification.

Prayer for Healing

The longest and most comprehensive passage on prayer in James's letter is found at the end of his correspondence. The relevant text is quoted in full below:

> Is anyone among you suffering? Let him pray. Is anyone cheerful? Let him sing praise. Is anyone among you sick? Let him call for the elders of the church, and let them pray over him, anointing him with oil in the name of the Lord. And the prayer of faith will save the one who is sick, and the Lord will raise him up. And if he has committed sins, he will be forgiven. Therefore, confess your sins to one another and pray for one another, that you may be healed. The prayer of a righteous person has great power as it is working. Elijah was a man with a nature like ours, and he prayed fervently that it might not rain, and for three years and six months it did not rain on

> the earth. Then he prayed again, and heaven gave rain, and the earth bore its fruit. (5:13–18)

This passage teaches us much about prayer: (1) Whatever circumstance one finds oneself in (i.e., suffering, joy, sickness), that exigency or feeling of gratitude should be directed back to God in prayer. (2) Christians should pray for one another, especially in times of desperate need, like serious illness. (3) Recognized leaders of the church have a special responsibility and obligation to pray for sick community members. Such prayer apparently is usually expected to involve more than one leader ("the elders of the church," 5:14). (4) Elder prayer for the healing of a congregant is also expected to be accompanied by anointing with oil. Such anointing mirrors the behavior of Jesus's disciples during his earthly ministry, when they anointed the sick for healing (Mark 6:13). (5) Christians should offer up prayer in faith for physical healing of the sick, believing that God is good, able, and kindly disposed to the petition. There should be a positive expectancy in the elders' prayer for healing. (6) It is possible that a community member's sickness may be a result of sin. Whether a community member is sick or not, it is always appropriate to confess one's sin and receive God's fatherly forgiveness. It can also be spiritually beneficial to confess sin to one another and reassure one another of God's grace in Christ. (7) The account of Elijah praying reminds us of what miraculous answers we can expect from our good and kind God, even as we remember our own weak creatureliness.

There are many other passages in the letter of James that do not explicitly mention prayer or asking God, but the Christian's activities described in those passages are most naturally understood as taking place in the context of prayer. For example, in James 4:1–10 the Christian is called to repent from "friendship with the world" (4:4) and to turn back to God: "Draw near to God, and he will draw near to you" (4:8). The most natural context in which this repentance and communication of godly sorrow can happen is in prayer. Indeed, virtually every paragraph in James invites the reader to respond to God in some way—faith, gratitude, repentance. The most natural context for such human-divine interaction is prayer.

Other Biblical Teaching on Prayer

Countless books have looked at the topic of prayer in the Bible. As we attempt to stay close with the prominent and explicit prayer-related topics in the letter of James, we will briefly consider representative Old Testament texts that teach the same thing.

One of the most prominent prayers for wisdom in the Old Testament is found in 1 Kings 3:6–9. In seeking help for his reign as king over Israel, Solomon asked God for wisdom. This pleased God, who responded to the petition:

> Because you have asked this, and have not asked for yourself long life or riches or the life of your enemies, but have asked for yourself understanding to discern what is right, behold, I now do according to your word. Behold, I give you a wise and discerning mind, so that none like you has been before you and none like you shall arise after you. (1 Kings 3:11–12)

After God rescued his people out of Egypt, they faced many practical needs over the next four decades, as they awaited their entrance to the promised land. When the Israelites grumbled and despaired rather than coming to God with their practical needs, they experienced judgment (Num. 11:1–2). When they asked God for help with practical needs—water (Ex. 15:25), food (Deut. 8:3), and victory in battle (Ex. 17:8–13)—he abundantly provided for his people.

Just as in the New Testament, the Old Testament describes God as having the power of life and death. He is able to heal any illness and even raise the dead. A poignant example of prayer for healing is found in Hannah's petition that the Lord would open her womb and enable her to have children (1 Sam. 1:1–20). The priest Eli declared to her, "Go in peace, and the God of Israel grant your petition that you have made to him" (1 Sam. 1:17).

The Gospels are replete with accounts of Jesus praying (e.g., Matt. 14:23; 26:36–39; Mark 1:35; 6:46; Luke 3:21; 5:16; 6:12) and of his teaching on prayer (e.g., Matt 6:5–13; 7:7–11; Luke 11:1–13). Throughout Jesus's teaching on prayer runs the theme that God's people should have an expectant attitude toward their heavenly Father's provision: "Ask, and it will be given to you; seek, and you will find; knock, and it will be opened to you. For everyone who asks receives, and the one who seeks finds, and to the one who knocks it will be opened" (Matt. 7:7–8). The Holy Spirit is the one who gives people wisdom and spiritual power for godliness, and Jesus assured his disciples, "If you then, who are evil, know how to give good gifts to your children, how much more will the heavenly Father give the Holy Spirit to those who ask him!" (Luke 11:13). In considering practical petitions for things like food and clothing, Jesus said,

> And why are you anxious about clothing? Consider the lilies of the field, how they grow: they neither toil nor spin, yet I tell you, even Solomon in all his glory was not arrayed like one of these. But if God so clothes the grass of the field, which today is alive and tomorrow is thrown into the oven, will he not much more clothe you, O you of little faith? (Matt. 6:28–30)

Since Jesus ascended to the right hand of God the Father, God's people now approach his throne in Jesus's name to bring their petitions for healing (James 5:14). During Jesus's earthly ministry, he could be approached and asked directly. The Gospels are filled with accounts of people who came to Jesus and asked for healing or who simply trusted in his power and goodness to heal. A woman who had been bleeding for twelve years was healed as she reached out and touched Jesus's garments. This is an example of a woman who acted in faith. Jesus told her, "Your faith has made you well" (Matt. 9:22).

The entire Bible is consistent in challenging God's people to pray in faith, to ask for wisdom and spiritual insight from God (Prov. 2:3–6; Jer. 33:3), to lift up practical needs to God (Ps. 81:10; Isa. 41:17), and to ask for healing (2 Chron. 7:14; Ps. 30:2)—while submitting all our petitions to his ultimate will (2 Sam. 15:25–26; Ps. 37:5; Prov. 3:5–6). The apostle Paul's prayer for physical healing from the thorn in his flesh (2 Cor. 12:8) provides an example of believing prayer for healing alongside submission to the divine will. God ultimately answered Paul's repeated petitions: "My grace is sufficient for you, for my power is made perfect in weakness" (2 Cor. 12:9).

Conclusion

Prayer is a significant theme in the letter of James. James instructs the recipients of his letter to pray for wisdom, practical needs, and healing. Indeed, James directs Christians to turn to God in prayer whatever one's situation or emotion, whether joy or suffering. This call for God's people to turn to him in all situations—trusting in his goodness, power, and loving concern—is reflected in all the Scriptures.

Conclusion

WHEN LOOKING AT A BIBLICAL TEXT, we are all prone to continue seeing the same things that we've previously observed. Readers of this volume have likely read through the letter of James many times. My hope, however, is that the previous chapters have helped you see more clearly the dominant themes in James and how these themes cohere with the rest of Scripture.

In obedience to the verses exposited above, I pause now to pray that God will give wisdom to you. I pray the Lord grants wisdom to understand his word, submit to it, and teach it faithfully to others. As you teach or preach through James, remember that his original audience would almost certainly have heard the letter in one sitting. Thus, if you exposit the text over several weeks or months, you should regularly remind your modern-day listeners of the Christological and soteriological underpinnings of the letter's practical paragraphs. Such emphasis on the priority of divine activity would have been fresh in the original listeners' ears as they pondered James's more practical exhortations. Let the same be true of us.

Acknowledgments

I'M GRATEFUL TO CROSSWAY, Tom Schreiner, and Brian Rosner for the invitation to write this volume. The keen eye and sharp mind of Crossway editor Chris Cowan significantly improved my work. The administration of Southern Seminary has always encouraged me in my scholarly pursuits, including the writing of this book. Thanks also to the seminary students over the last two decades who took my class on the Greek exegesis of James. Their questions and insights have improved my understanding of the letter. Dave DeKlavon, Daniel Kunkel, and Bradley Jessup read an earlier draft of the manuscript and offered helpful edits. I'm grateful for my lovely wife Chandi and three daughters Sarah, Chloe, and Anabelle, who are always in my heart and mind. Finally, to the triune God, who called this unworthy sinner into his service: I kneel before you, my sovereign, and offer this volume as an act of worship.

Recommended Resources

Commentaries

Adam, A. K. M. *James. A Handbook on the Greek Text*. Baylor University Press, 2013.

Davids, Peter H. *The Epistle of James*. NIGTC. Eerdmans, 1982.

McCartney, Dan G. *James*. BECNT. Baker Academic, 2009.

Moo, Douglas J. *The Letter of James*. PNTC. Eerdmans, 2000.

Plummer, Robert L. *James*. In *Hebrews–Revelation*, 219–86. Vol. 12 of *ESV Expository Commentary*. Edited by Iain M. Duguid, James M. Hamilton Jr., and Jay Sklar. Crossway, 2018.

Varner, William. *James: A Commentary on the Greek Text*. Fontes, 2017.

Vlachos, Chris A. *James*. EGGNT. B&H Academic, 2013.

Theological Volumes and Focused Studies

Bauckham, Richard. *James: Wisdom of James, Disciple of Jesus the Sage*. New Testament Readings. Routledge, 1999.

Cheung, Luke Leuk. *The Genre, Composition, and Hermeneutics of the Epistle of James*. Paternoster Biblical Monographs. Reprint, Wipf and Stock, 2006.

Davids, Peter. *A Theology of James, Peter, and Jude: Living in the Light of the Coming King*. BTNT. Zondervan Academic, 2014.

Hartin, Patrick. *A Spirituality of Perfection: Faith in Action in the Letter of James*. Liturgical, 1999.

Johnson, Luke Timothy. *Brother of Jesus, Friend of God: Studies in the Letter of James*. Eerdmans, 2004.

Laato, Timo. "Justification According to James: A Comparison with Paul." *Trinity Journal* 18, no. 1 (1997): 43–84.

General Index

Scripture Index

New Testament Theology

The Beginning of the Gospel
MARK

From the Manger to the Throne
LUKE

The Mission of the Triune God
ACTS

Strengthened by the Gospel
ROMANS

Ministry in the New Realm
2 CORINTHIANS

Christ Crucified
GALATIANS

United to Christ, Walking in the Spirit
EPHESIANS

Sharing Christ in Joy and Sorrow
PHILIPPIANS

Hidden with Christ in God
COLOSSIANS AND PHILEMON

To Walk and to Please God
1 AND 2 THESSALONIANS

The Appearing of God Our Savior
1 AND 2 TIMOTHY AND TITUS

Perfect Priest for Weary Pilgrims
HEBREWS

Living Faith
JAMES

The God Who Judges and Saves
2 PETER AND JUDE

The Joy of Hearing
REVELATION

Edited by Thomas R. Schreiner and Brian S. Rosner, this series presents clear, scholarly overviews of the main theological themes of each book of the New Testament, examining what they reveal about God and his relation to the world in the context of the overarching biblical narrative.